Zabalin

Anno Wilms
Zabalin
Die Müllmenschen von Mokattam, Cairo

mit Textbeiträgen von
Christine Bücking
und Claus Kühne

edition **CON**

CIP-Kurztitelaufnahme der Deutschen Bibliothek
Wilms, Anno:
Zabalin: d. Müllmenschen von Mokattam, Cairo /
Anno Wilms. Texte von Christine Bücking u.
Claus Kühne. – 1. Aufl. – Bremen: Edition CON, 1985.
ISBN 3-88526-046-8
NE: Bücking, Christine (Mitarb.)

Lektorat: Erich Czichy
Umschlag und Layout: Piet Claassen
Satz: Composer-Studio M.-I. Könnecke
Herstellung: Perspektiven, Bremen
© by CON Medien- und Vertriebsgesellschaft mbH, Bremen
Alle Rechte vorbehalten
1. Auflage 1985
Printed in West Germany
ISBN 3-88526-046-8

Inhalt

Müll in Cairo

Anmerkungen zur Geschichte der Stadt

Wie überall wurde früher auch in Kairo der anfallende Hausmüll wiederverwertet, denn die Haushalte besaßen Tiere, an die die organischen Abfälle verfüttert wurden, und sie verheizten das brennbare Material in den Öfen. Müll als ein wertloses und zu beseitigendes Abfallprodukt entstand erst durch die Europäisierung bestimmter Stadtteile und den dadurch veränderten Lebensstandard. Diese begann in der zweiten Hälfte des 19. Jahrhunderts (abgesehen von den ersten europäischen Einflüssen Napoleons) mit dem Suezkanalbau, dem Baumwollboom, dem Kreditwesen und der Landspekulation.

Die französische Sprache und Kultur, die Ideen, die Diplomatie – vor allem aber die wirtschaftlichen Aktivitäten – der europäischen Kolonialmächte verdrängten die zu dieser Zeit herrschenden Osmanen. Für Großbritannien war Cairo von strategisch wichtiger Bedeutung als Zwischenstation von und nach Indien. Zur Durchsetzung ihrer wirtschaftlichen Interessen überzogen die Engländer zudem den nördlichen Teil des Landes mit einer Infrastruktur, um Baumwolle und andere Produkte schneller und sicherer fortzuschaffen.

1872 lebten dreihunderttausend Menschen in Cairo. Von den fünfundachtzigtausend Ausländern, die sich in der Stadt niedergelassen hatten, waren etwa ein Drittel Europäer. Das Straßenbild änderte sich zusehends. Italienische, griechische, französische und englische Stadtviertel und Gartenstädte entstanden. Breite Boulevards und große Rondelle mit sternförmig auseinanderlaufenden Straßen durchzogen die neuen Viertel. Ismael, der vorletzte osmanische Herrscher, träumte von einem 'Paris am Nil', für das er sich allerdings so sehr verschuldete, daß die europäischen Kolonialmächte seine Abdankung erzwingen konnten. Unaufhaltsam wuchs im Westen entlang des Nils und auf den Inseln Gezirah und Rodah eine moderne europäische Stadt mit den architektonischen Spielereien aus „1001 Nacht". Alles, was die europäische Kolonie für ihr Wohlbefinden und Vergnügen brauchte, holte sie sich in die Stadt. Ein neuer Vorort, Heliopolis, entstand, geplant nur für Europäer. Es gab Straßenbahnlinien und Vorortbahnen, Pferdekutschen, englische

und französische Tageszeitungen, ein Opernhaus, Clubs, Golf-
plätze, Pferderennbahnen, Zigarrengeschäfte usw.
Gleichzeitig entwickelten sich neue soziale Gepflogenheiten. Die
gehobene Mittelklasse brachte einen neuen Typus von Geschäfts-
leuten hervor, die neue Formen von Korruption und Ausbeutung ein-
führten. Der Baumwollboom von 1903 versetzte die Stadt in eine Art
Goldrausch. Die feudalen Landbesitzer, die ihre Gewinne noch nicht
in Industrie und Handel steckten, gaben viel Geld in Cairo aus, ließen
sich prachtvolle Villen bauen und versuchten am englischen Lebens-
stil teilzuhaben.

Die Hierarchie in der Gesellschaft war festgefügt: Die reichen Engländer sahen herab auf die weniger reichen, alle Engländer wiederum
auf die übrigen Ausländer. Diese Ausländer mißachteten gemeinsam
alle Ägypter, und die reichen Ägypter wähnten sich besser als die
mittelständischen. Verbunden waren alle in ihrer gemeinsamen Ver-
achtung der Fellachen, die den Großteil der Reichtümer schufen und
deren Rücken sich unter der Last dieser Pyramide krümmen mußte.

Während der großen baulichen Aktivitäten im Westen der Stadt blieb
der Osten, umgeben von der mächtigen Stadtmauer mit den Hand-
werkervierteln und dem Bazar, mittelalterlich arabisch! Im Norden,
Osten und Süden der Stadt entstanden die Wohnsiedlungen der
armen Bevölkerung, die vom Lande in die Stadt strömte.
Zu dieser Zeit hatte sich die Einwohnerzahl Cairos binnen fünfund-
zwanzig Jahren verdoppelt. Sechshundertfünfundfünfzigtausend
Menschen lebten 1907 in der Stadt. Vor allem anderen waren dafür
die „Beschäftigungsprobleme" in den Provinzen auf dem Lande ver-
antwortlich, nicht etwa eine übergroße Zunahme der Geburten.
Unter der Regie der Kolonialherren war die Landwirtschaft auf
Monokultur und Cashcrops (z. B. Baumwolle) umgestellt worden.
Die damit verbundene große Abhängigkeit vom Weltmarkt brachte
infolge periodischer Absatzschwierigkeiten tausende der Landarbei-
ter und Bauern um ihr täglich Brot. Der Hunger trieb sie nach Cairo;
dort konnte man billige Arbeitskräfte für jene niederen Arbeiten gut
gebrauchen, die eine großstädtische Entwicklung nach den Leitbil-

dern der „herrschenden ausländischen Kolonie" mit sich brachte.
Der Bauboom und die vielseitigen neuen Aufgaben, die in Cairo
gelöst werden mußten, absorbierten einen Teil der Landflüchtigen.
Andere drängten in die vornehmen europäischen Viertel der Stadt, in
der Hoffnung, mit den Ausländern Handel treiben zu können. Alle
erdenklichen Dienstleistungen wurden den Reichen der Stadt ange-
boten.
Zum Beispiel die der Hausmüllbeseitigung!
Es war ein Müllproblem entstanden, wie man es bis dahin in Cairo
erst kurze Zeit kannte und für dessen Bewältigung ungeplant – eben
naturwüchsig, anarchisch, sozusagen der Not gehorchend – eine
funktionale Struktur entstehen sollte.

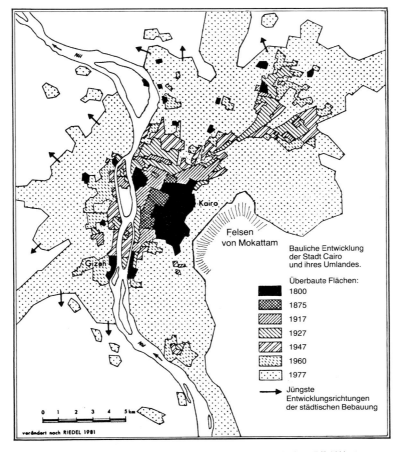

Bauliche Ausdehnung Cairos seit 1800   Aus geogr. Rundschau 5/84 Westermann

Zabalin
Zwei völlig verschiedene Bevölkerungsgruppen

Wahis

Charga und Dakhla sind zwei Oasen in der südlichen Libyschen Wüste. Auch Bewohner dieser, von der landwirtschaftlichen Umstellung nicht betroffenen Gebiete setzten sich vor ungefähr hundert Jahren Richtung Cairo in Bewegung, auf der Suche nach Arbeit. Genaue Gründe für das Verlassen ihrer Dörfer sind nicht festzustellen.

Da in Oasen Brunnen periodisch versiegen, ebenso Quellen, die manchmal nach vielen Jahren andernorts wieder sprudeln, gehen wir davon aus, daß dies einer der Gründe war, die Heimat zu verlassen. Hinzukommt, daß die Instandhaltung der Brunnen und unterirdischen Kanäle lebensgefährlich und äußerst aufwendig war und mit der Zeit zunehmend vernachlässigt wurde. Ein weiterer Anlaß mögen die rigorosen Wasserrechte gewesen sein, die es weniger einflußreichen Bauern unmöglich machten, ihre Nutzfläche zu erhalten oder gar zu erweitern.

Um sich in Cairo eine Existenzgrundlage zu schaffen, nahmen sich diese Menschen der aufkommenden Müllproblematik an und entsorgten die neuen Stadtgebiete regelmäßig. Sie sammelten die Abfälle, die meist noch rein organisch waren, trockneten sie und verkauften die Fladen an Bäckereien, Tonbrennereien und türkische Badehäuser, die damit das Badewasser erwärmten.*

Die Nachfahren dieser ersten Müllarbeiter von Cairo, die sich Wahis oder Zaballa nannten (zibal = Abfall), leben auch heute noch als eine in sich geschlossene Gruppe in einem bestimmten Cairoer Viertel unweit des Hauptbahnhofs. Das Geschäft mit dem Müll dürfte recht einträglich gewesen sein, denn die Wahis achteten von Anfang an auf eine genaue Organisation. Jede Familie hatte eigene Routen, die

---

* Brennbare Abfälle werden auch heute noch in den wenigen existierenden Badehäusern verheizt, um das Wasser zu wärmen. Die Energie wird dabei mehrfach genutzt: heiße Asche wird in Erdkuhlen vor den Ofen geschüttet, in welche vorher fest verschlossene kupferne Gefäße mit dem Grundnahrungsmittel Fool gestellt wurden. Dieses Bohnengericht gart über Nacht und wird am Morgen von Straßenhändlern verkauft.

bedient wurden. Um Neubauten wurde gefeilscht. Die Routen blieben im Familienbesitz und die Kinder übernahmen das Geschäft der Eltern. Das ständig wachsende Cairo erstickte auf diese Weise nicht am Müll und das holzarme Land konnte mit billigem Brennstoff versorgt werden.

Zabalin

Gewaltsame Landvertreibung durch Feudalherren verursachte im frühen 19. Jahrhundert große Not in Ägypten. Viele Bauern konnten in weniger fruchtbaren Jahren die Pacht für ihre kleinen Parzellen nicht erwirtschaften. Sie gerieten an die örtlichen Geldverleiher, die durch Wucherzinsen dafür sorgten, daß das Heer landloser Bauern gewaltig anschwoll; wie es den Interessen des sich neu orientierenden Großgrundbesitzes entsprach. Man verfügte jetzt über beliebig viele Wanderarbeiter, die sich hervorragend für die Baumwollwirtschaft nutzen ließen.

Allerdings sichert der Baumwollanbau eine Beschäftigung nur bei Aussaat und Ernte. Dieses Tarahilsystem gibt es auch heute noch. Für die männlichen Jugendlichen war die saisonale Unterbeschäftigung häufig Grund genug, den dörflichen Raum zu verlassen. Über Provinzhauptstädte, die auch nicht genügend Arbeitsplätze boten, zogen sie in der Hoffnung auf eine Beschäftigung nach Cairo.

Für Kopten, christliche Ägypter (etwa 8 % bis 10 % der Bevölkerung), die aus Oberägypten nach Cairo migrierten, stellten sich zusätzliche Probleme. Wie andere mittellose Zuwanderer auch, siedelten sie am Rand der Stadt. Eine Eingliederung in die städtische islamische Bevölkerung war aber selbst perspektivisch gar nicht möglich wegen der von ihnen betriebenen Schweinezucht.
Das Futter für die Schweine bezogen sie von den Wahis. Abnehmer für das Fleisch fanden sie bei den Ausländern und – natürlich – der koptischen Gemeinde. So entwickelten sich im Lauf der Zeit viele kleine Zuchtbetriebe in diesen fast ausschließlich von koptischen Zuwanderern bewohnten Siedlungen.
Die Wahis, ihre Futterlieferanten, hatten sich mittlerweile etabliert und vermieteten nach und nach ihre Müllrouten an die Kopten, die sich Zabalin* nennen. Diese beiden Gruppen, die Wahis und die

* Der Name 'Zabalin' ist verwirrend, da sich auch die Wahis so nennen. So ist es nicht verwunderlich, daß den meisten Cairenern der Unterschied zwischen beiden Gruppen nicht bekannt ist. Ein anderer Name für die schweinezüchtenden Müllsammler ist Zarrab (arab. Zeriba – Schweinestall, Haus und Hof), der aber nicht sehr geläufig ist. Im folgenden benutzen wir die Bezeichnung Zabalin.

Zabalin, entwickelten ein komplexes System von geschäftlichen Beziehungen, das bis heute seine Gültigkeit hat und die Hausmüll- abfuhr von Cairo garantiert, welche noch immer vollständig privat organisiert ist.

Die Beziehung zwischen Zabalin und Wahis

Die Wahis kaufen von einem Hausbesitzer das Recht, den Müll abzu-
holen. Dieses Recht besteht, solange das Haus existiert und wird
innerhalb der Wahifamilie weitervererbt. Früher war die Zahlung des
Wahis an den Hausbesitzer einmalig und betrug je nach Größe 25
bis 100 L.E.* Heute werden für große Apartementhäuser 1000 bis
2000 L.E. bezahlt, und in einigen Fällen sichert sich der Wahi durch
zusätzliche Zahlungen ab. Von den Mietern der Wohnungen kassiert
er eine monatliche Gebühr, und zwar je nach Wohngegend, Miete
und Status 0.25 bis 1.– L.E.

Der Wahi überläßt den Müll einem Zabalin, der diesen täglich aus den
Wohnungen abholt. Für eine Route mit ungefähr dreihundert bis vierhundert Wohnungen muß der Zabalin an den Wahi eine bestimmte
Summe bezahlen, die sich an der Wohngegend und somit auch an
der Qualität des Abfalls orientiert. Eine gute Route bezahlt er mit bis
zu 1000 L.E., die er in monatlichen Raten tilgen kann.
Dafür kann der Zabalin über den gesamten Müll verfügen. Organische Abfälle werden an die Schweine verfüttert, wiederverwendba-
res Material wird gesammelt und an Altwarenhändler, die Moalems,
verkauft. Der Wahi ist zum Müllmakler geworden. Er organisiert, ver-
waltet, garantiert für die Abholung und kassiert, während der Zabalin
die wirkliche Arbeit verrichtet. Er zieht täglich mit seinem Eselskarren
durch die Straßen der Stadt und läuft oft bis in die fünfte und sechste
Etage, um die Abfälle, die dort vor der Tür stehen, einzusammeln.

Durch das komplizierte Aufteilungssystem der Wahis liegen die Häuser einer Route nicht in einem Straßenzug, sondern über ein ganzes
Stadtviertel verteilt. Die Zabalin dürfen Routen untereinander nicht
tauschen, sondern die gehen immer wieder zurück in die Verfügung
der Wahis.
Zur Sicherung ihrer Interessen besitzen die Wahis eine eigene straffe
Organisation, die jede Einmischung von außen verhindert. So haben

---

* Der Wechselkurs für 1 L.E. beträgt derzeit durchschnittlich 2,05 DM.

Anwärter außerhalb des Wahiclans keine Chance, in das Müllgeschäft einzusteigen. Streitigkeiten untereinander schlichten sie über ihre Organisation und nach Darstellung von Beobachtern unter Umständen auch durch Stockkämpfe.

Die Menschen

vor den
Felsen
von Mokattam

Bei unserem ersten Besuch sind wir zu Fuß unterwegs. Die öffentlichen Verkehrsverbindungen reichen nur bis zu der großen Ausfallstraße, von dort aus sind es noch ungefähr 5 km durch eines der vielen Squattergebiete Cairos. Erst am Rande dieses Viertels hat man den Blick frei auf die Siedlung der Müllmenschen.*

Von weitem unterscheidet sie sich kaum von den eben durchquerten eng bebauten kleinen Straßenzügen mit selbsterrichteten Häusern aus Stein und ehemaligen Ölfässern oder Bretterbuden. Inmitten der Siedlung fällt der solide Backsteinbau der koptischen Kirche ins Auge. Verschiedentlich sieht man freie, nicht bebaute Plätze. Dort stapeln sich die recycelbaren Materialien: Stoff, Papier, Blech usw. Graue Rauchschwaden am Rande deuten auf die vielen kleinen Brandherde hin, durch die der liegengebliebene Müll verringert werden soll.

Die Bewohner der ersten Häuser an der Eingangsstraße der Siedlung haben eine Art Kontrollfunktion. Sie fragen fremde Personen nach dem Grund ihres Besuches und verweigern je nach Ermessen den Einlaß.

Daß man uns nicht gleich an den ersten Häusern der Siedlung wieder zurückschickte, haben wir nur der Überredungskunst unseres Freundes und Übersetzers Haschim zu verdanken.

* Das Bauland um Cairo ist knapp und teuer. Wenn für Spekulanten – aber auch die Behörden – profitable Nutzung solcher Gegenden möglich erschien, nahm man auf die Menschen, die zwar real aber nicht juristisch dort lebten, wenig Rücksicht. Dies betraf mehrfach die Zabalin. 1972 wurde eine große Siedlung im Nordwesten der Stadt evakuiert. Damals zwang man die Zabalin, ihren Hausstand binnen vier Tagen aufzulösen. Da ein Schweineherdentransport durch das moslemische Cairo undenkbar gewesen wäre, mußten die Tiere weit unter Preis notverkauft werden. Ungefähr vierhundert Familien zogen um, quer durch die Stadt. Ihr neuer, ihnen zugewiesener Ort lag im Osten jenseits des großen Khalifenfriedhofes (der „Totenstadt"). Diese Lage ist günstiger als alle bisherigen Wohnorte der Müllmenschen: es ist die große steinige Ebene direkt vor den Felsen von Mokattam. Dorthin wird sich die Stadt nicht mehr ausdehnen können; denn das Felsmassiv mit seiner Steilkante bildet eine natürliche Grenze.

Unser erster Eindruck, noch geprägt von den Sauberkeitserfahrungen und Ordnungsvorstellungen der Heimat, war erschlagend. Müll, Dreck und Elend solchen Ausmaßes betäubte. Erst langsam veränderte sich unser Verhältnis zum Müll, und wir konnten die Wohn- und Arbeitsbedingungen der Menschen differenzierter wahrnehmen, die von und mit dieser Ware leben.

Es ist Frühjahr und noch nicht so heiß, jedoch sehr windig. Bäume oder anderen Schutz vor dem Wind, der aus der nahen Wüste herüberweht, gibt es nicht. Man kann vielleicht zweihundertfünfzig Meter weit sehen. Alles ist gelb-grau verschleiert. Wir gehen durch liegengebliebenes und verwehtes Papier und Plastik, rostige Dosen und Schweinemist und machen einen Bogen um ein zerfetztes totes Schwein, das ungezählte Fliegen umschwirren.
Die Straßen sind eng bebaut. Ehemals freie Plätze füllen bereits neue Zeribas*; wie überall in Cairo wird auch hier der Wohnraum knapp. Es herrscht reges Treiben. Vor den Häusern spielen die Kinder, die Frauen kaufen ein oder bringen recycelbares Material zu den Sammelstellen und unterhalten sich mit den anderen. Eselskarren, beladen oder leer, holpern die Wege entlang. Der Gemüsehändler mit dem Handkarren bietet lauthals seine Ware an, der LKW des Stoffhändlers fährt die Straße herunter. Auch in diesem Viertel gibt es Teehäuser, von denen aus die Männer bei Wasserpfeife und Tee die Szenerie der Straße beobachten können.

Im Gegensatz zum Mißtrauen bei der Eingangskontrolle hat uns bei diesem und allen späteren Besuchen besonders die große Gastfreundschaft der Zabalin beeindruckt. Immer wieder wurden wir in die Zeribas hineingewunken zu einer Tasse Tee und zu Fragen nach unserem Namen, woher wir kämen und wieviele Kinder wir denn hätten. So hatten wir ausführlich Gelegenheit, uns eine Zeriba von innen anzusehen.

* Zeriba: Haus, Hof und Schweinestall

26

Die Wohnsituation

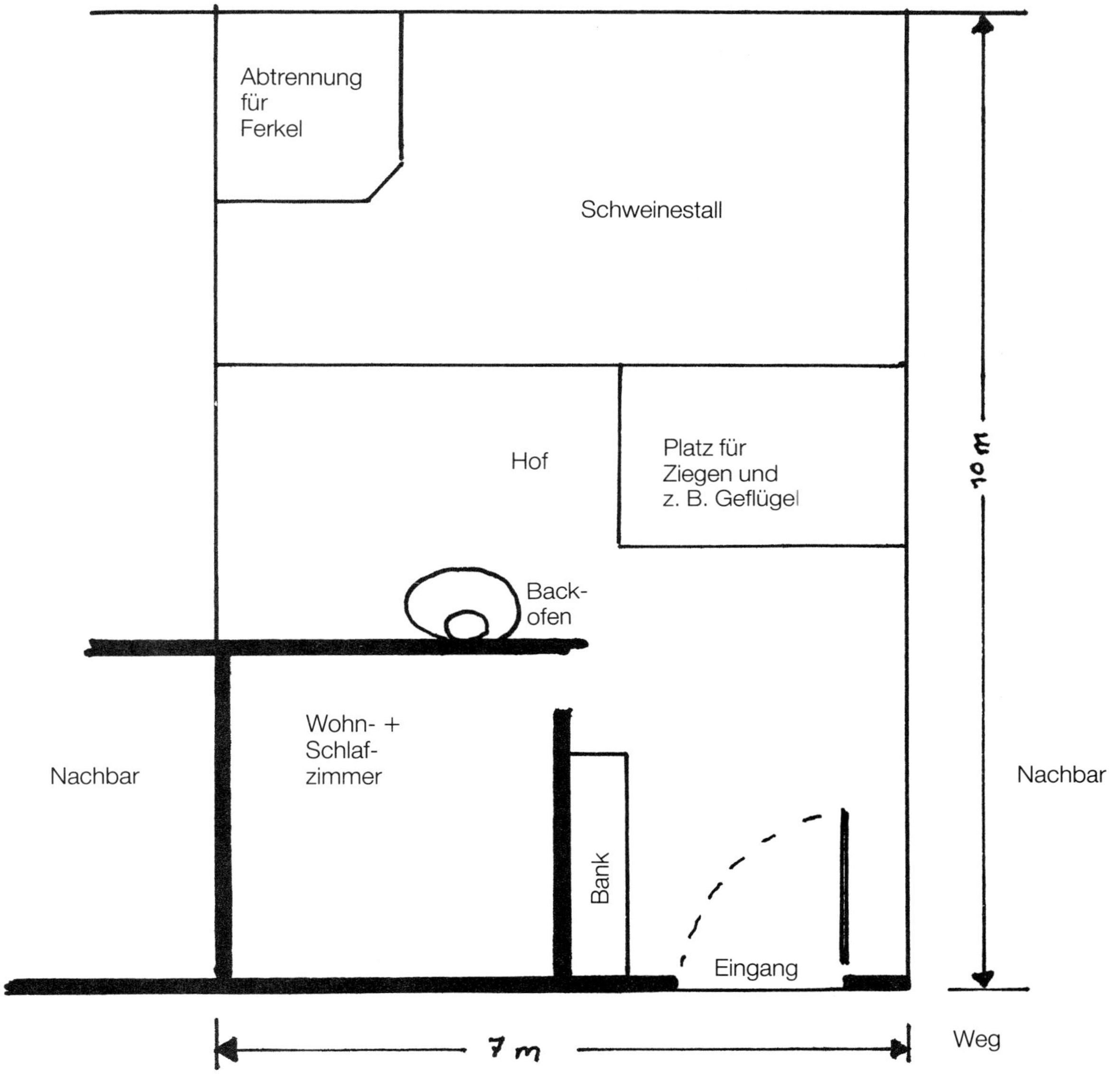

Abtrennung
für
Ferkel

Schweinestall

Hof

Platz für
Ziegen und
z. B. Geflügel

Back-
ofen

Wohn- +
Schlaf-
zimmer

Nachbar

Bank

Eingang

Nachbar

10 m

7 m

Weg

Haus, Hof und Schweinestall sind alle nach dem gleichen Muster gebaut.

27

Der Platz vor dem Haus auf der Straße gilt als Erweiterung des Wohnraums; dort sitzen die Frauen zusammen. Die Eingangstür ist häufig weit offen für den Eselskarren. Im vorderen Teil des Hofes sortieren die Frauen die Karrenladung; organische Abfälle als Futter für die Schweine; recycelbares Material wird in verschiedenen Behältern gesammelt und je nach Menge alle paar Tage an die Händler der Siedlung verkauft. Hinten im Hof wird gewaschen, gekocht und gegessen. Meist gibt es einen kleinen gemauerten Ofen, in dem einmal wöchentlich das ägyptische Fladenbrot 'aish baladi', die Grundnahrung der armen Bevölkerung, gebacken wird. Haustiere wie Ziegen, Geflügel oder auch Wasserbüffel leben ebenfalls im hinteren Teil des Hofes. Einer oder mehrere Schlafräume begrenzen den Hof zur Straße hin. Kleine Fenster lassen ein wenig Licht hinein. Die Einrichtung besteht hauptsächlich aus Schlafgelegenheiten: Betten, Matrazen, Zudecken, manchmal ein Sofa, selten Tisch und Stühle, denn das Familienleben findet draußen statt. Hinterm Hof, oft nur durch eine Blechwand abgetrennt, ist der Schweinestall, den auch die Esel mitbenutzen. Dort werden im Durchschnitt dreißig Schweine aufgezogen, die zwei- bis dreimal jährlich von einem der großen Schweinehändler aufgekauft werden.*

* Die Schweinezucht ist die ökonomische Grundlage eines jeden Betriebes, da das Schwein ein optimaler Futterverwerter ist. Zwar gibt es in den Zeribas meistens auch ein paar Ziegen, aber diese Tiere sind nicht schon nach sechs bis acht Monaten verkaufsreif wie die Schweine. So sind auch einige der Moslems, die in den Siedlungen als kleine Minderheit existieren, zur Schweinezucht übergegangen. Ein religiöses Tabu wich ökonomischen Zwängen. Mit den organischen Abfällen einer Eselskarrenladung Müll pro Tag (etwa 700 kg) lassen sich etwa dreißig Schweine, fünf Ziegen und zwei Esel ernähren. Dies ist auch die häufigste Größe des Betriebes einer Zabalinfamilie. Betrieben wird hier Schweinezucht und nicht Mast. Zabalin besitzen mehrere Säue, ein oder zwei Eber und verkaufen zwei- bis dreimal im Jahr die Ferkel an spezielle Mastbetriebe. Der Erlös aus dieser Arbeit dürfte durchschnittlich bei 3.– L.E. je Tag liegen. (Die dagegenstehenden Kosten sind weiter hinten aufgeführt.)

Insbesondere durch die Öffentlichkeits- und Sozialarbeit der koptischen Kirche hat sich die Wohnsituation der Zabalin in Mokattam im Laufe der letzten zehn Jahre stabilisiert. Während sie bisher ständig mit der Gefahr der plötzlichen Vertreibung rechnen mußten und somit auch ein relativ unbeteiligtes Verhältnis zu ihrer Wohngegend entwickelten, haben sie nun die Möglichkeit, sich eine Existenz aufzubauen. Zwei Drittel der Blechhütten in Mokattam sind bereits durch Steinhäuser ersetzt worden, eine Investition, die die Zabalinfamilie 250–300 L.E. kostet. Nicht entwickelt hat sich demgegenüber die Infrastruktur. Es gibt keine öffentliche Schule, keinen Kooperativladen mit einem Angebot von subventionierten Waren, keine medizinische Versorgung, keine Apotheke und kein Krankenhaus. Der größte Mangel allerdings sind fehlende Wasserversorgung und Kanlalisation. Eine solche Situation findet man kaum in einem anderen Viertel Cairos.*

* Diese katastrophale Vernachlässigung von Existenzgrundlagen einer Wohnsiedlung läßt Rückschlüsse auf die soziale Stellung der Zabalin, sowohl in den Augen der übrigen Bevölkerung als auch bei Regierungskreisen zu. Verkehrsplaner haben 1980 ein Gesetz erwirkt, das den Zabalin das Mülleinsammeln während des Tages verbietet, da die vielen Eselskarren den Verkehr behindern. Falls sie jetzt am Tage von einem Polizisten gesehen werden (und für die Müllsammler ist es unvermeidlich, wenigstens eine Strecke während des Tages zurückzulegen), müssen sie ein zusätzliches Backschisch abgeben, um so einer größeren Strafe zu entgehen. Man kann dieses Gesetz als eine Möglichkeit zur Aufbesserung des schlechten Polizistenlohns verstehen, denn verändert hat sich in der Praxis gar nichts; die Zabalinkarren gehören zum Cairoer Straßenbild wie die überfüllten, auseinanderbrechenden roten Stadtbusse . . . Weitere Probleme schafft die Nachtarbeit der Zabalin. Die allgemeine soziale Stigmatisierung der Müllmenschen innerhalb der Bevölkerung bekommt Nahrung, denn es werden automatisch immer die Zabalinkinder verdächtigt, etwas gestohlen oder kaputtgemacht zu haben. Wie überall auf der Welt ist die Arbeit mit dem Müll als schmutzig und minderwertig verpönt. Und nicht nur die Arbeit, auch die Ausführenden gelten als minderwertig.

Unter den Bewohnern von Mokattam gibt es eine Gruppe, die gar nicht oder nur indirekt mit dem Müll-Geschäft zu tun hat. Es sind die diversen Geschäftebesitzer, die Teehausinhaber und die mobilen Verkäufer, die auf Handwagen Waren und Dienstleistungen aller Art anbieten.

Eine andere Möglichkeit, sein Geld zu verdienen, demonstriert uns Said, Verbindungsmann zwischen dem Schweinegroßhändler Morcos und den Zabalin. Er hat sich ein Ladegerät für Autobatterien angeschafft, und um sein Bett im Schlafzimmer türmen sich die Autobatterien, mit denen die bessergestellten Zabalin ihre Fernseher betreiben.

Über die wirklichen Lebens- und Arbeitsbedingungen der Zabalin wissen nur wenige Einheimische Bescheid, wie auch nur einigen Ägyptern die Existenz und Bedeutung des weitverzweigten Recyclingmarktes bekannt ist. Die Zabalin ihrerseits sind verbittert über die mangelnde Anerkennung ihrer für die Gesamtbevölkerung so wichtigen Arbeit.

Obwohl überall in der Siedlung Müll herumliegt, ist es keine Müllkippe, auf der die Menschen leben. Der gesammelte Hausmüll wird in die Zeribas hereingeholt und bis auf ungefähr fünf Prozent verarbeitet.

Auch sind die Zabalin keine 'entwurzelten' oder 'asozialen Elemente', die – untereinander in Konkurrenzdruck – sich aus dem Dreck der anderen Menschen noch etwas zum Leben heraussuchen. Es bestehen ein soziales Netz von gegenseitiger Hilfeleistung und Unterstützung, enge familiäre Beziehungen und anhaltende Kontakte zur heimatlichen Gegend um Assiut (Oberägypten). Dies sind ein wesentlicher Teil der Voraussetzungen dafür, daß sich das Geschäft mit dem Müll überhaupt so weit entwickelt hat, wie wir es heute vorfinden.

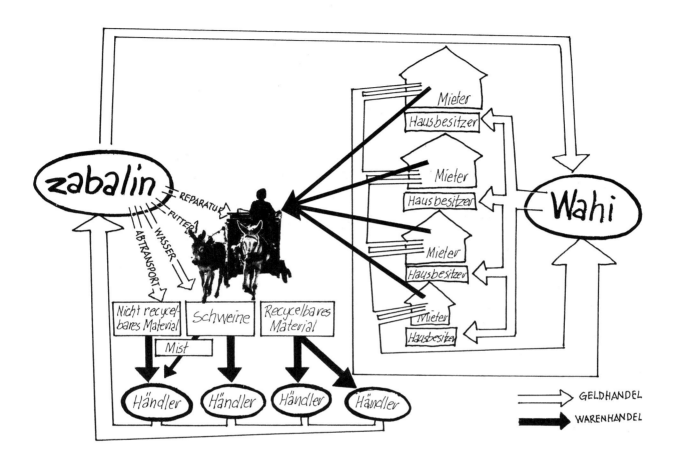

zabalin

REPARATUR
FUTTER
WASSER
ABTRANSPORT

Nicht recycel-bares Material

Mist

Schweine

Recycelbares Material

Händler   Händler   Händler   Händler

Mieter
Hausbesitzer

Mieter
Hausbesitzer

Mieter
Hausbesitzer

Mieter
Hausbesitzer

Wahi

GELDHANDEL

WARENHANDEL

Familie
und
die Teilung
der Arbeit

Die Kinder – im Durchschnitt sechs pro Familie – nehmen abwechselnd an den täglichen Touren teil. Meist sind es die Mädchen im Alter zwischen vier und zwölf Jahren, die man im Straßenverkehr auf dem Kutscherbock den Eselskarren lenken sieht. Eine Mülltour erfordert in der Regel drei Arbeitskräfte: die kleinen Kinder zwischen vier und sieben Jahren sitzen im Karren und passen auf, daß niemand die Esel stiehlt, denn sie sind eines der wichtigsten Produktionsmittel der Zabalin. Die anderen beiden gehen von Haus zu Haus und sammeln den bereitgestellten Müll der einzelnen Mieter in einen großen Korb, den sie im Eselskarren entleeren. Dies sind meist die älteren Kinder; je nach Familiengröße auch die jugendlichen oder erwachsenen Söhne. Auf dem Nachhauseweg quer durch den ewigen Verkehrsstau wird der Müll ein erstes Mal nach kleinen Schätzen und anderen Nützlichkeiten durchsucht. Insbesondere die Mädchen fallen durch allerlei Halskettchen und Ringe, durch viel zu große Hakkenschuhe und kleine Handtaschen mit abgerissenen Henkeln auf.*

Die Dauer einer Tour beträgt im Durchschnitt acht Stunden pro Tag, wobei zwei Drittel der Zeit im Verkehr verlorengeht. Oft fahren die Kinder vor Morgengrauen los, um wenigstens eine Tour ohne Verkehrschaos zurücklegen zu können. Wieder in Mokattam angelangt, kommt es manchmal vor, daß die zwei Esel es nicht schaffen, den vollbeladenen Karren den Berg hochzuziehen. Dann muß aus der Zeriba ein weiterer Esel zur Verstärkung geholt werden. Zuhause angekommen, muß Wasser besorgt werden. Die Esel werden vor einen Tankwagen gespannt und diejenigen Kinder, die den Tag über zuhause oder in der Schule waren, müssen 3 km bis zur nächsten Siedlung fahren, um Familie und Tiere mit Wasser zu versorgen.

* Neben der Schweinezucht ist der Erlös aus dem Verkauf aussortierter Materialien die zweite Einnahmequelle der Zabalin. Die Ausbeute ist von Tag zu Tag so unterschiedlich, daß genaue Zahlen schwerlich zu nennen sind. Jeder Zabalin wird die Frage nach guten Funden verneinen und trotzdem weiter von versehentlich weggeworfenen Schätzen träumen. Die eine oder andere Armbanduhr zeugt von einem derartigen Glückstreffer! Aber der Alltag, gekennzeichnet durch das Sortieren der wiederverwertbaren Materialien, ist hart und die Ausbeute gering.

Das Wasser stellt ein großes Problem in der Siedlung dar. Die koptische Kirche hat zwar einen kleinen Hahn, der aber den großen Bedarf bei weitem nicht decken kann. Im Sommer brauchen die Tiere, besonders die Schweine, viel Wasser, da sie sonst reihenweise an Hitzschlag sterben. Doch gerade im Sommer, wo der tägliche Familienbedarf bei einer Tankfüllung von 180 l liegt, bricht die überlastete Wasserversorgung oft zusammen. Die öffentlichen Brunnen, die cirka fünfzigtausend Menschen einschließlich der zehntausend Zabalin versorgen sollen, sind trocken, weil die Wasserleitung vorher irgendwo ein Leck hat, aus dem ein kleiner Springbrunnen die lehmigen Straßen überflutet. Das bedeutet für die Zabalinkinder eine lange Fahrt gen Norden; spätestens am Flughafen 10 km weiter, können sie dann ihr Wasser kaufen.

* Hier eine Tabelle, die uns über die durchschnittliche Zusammensetzung des Mülls berichtet, je nachdem, welcher sozialen Schicht die Müllieferanten zuzuordnen wären.

Müllzusammensetzung	Ober-	% Mittel- Schicht	Unter-
Verwertbare org. Abfälle (Gemüse usw.)	75	72	27
gemischtes Papier	16	14,5	10
gemischtes Glas	3	2,5	1
Textilien und Knochen	2	4,5	1,5
eisenhaltiges Metall und Konservendosen	2	1,5	–
gemischtes Plastik	0,6	0,2	–
Kupfer	0,01	0,01	–
Aluminium	0,09	–	–
Batterien (Zink)	0,02	0,15	–
nicht verwertbare Abfälle (Schmutz, Fäkalien usw.)	1,35	4,64	60,5
Summe	100	100	100

Bei einer Karrenladung wären das z. B. ganze 21 kg Glas. Für eine Tonne unsortiertes Altglas bezahlt der Kleinhändler in der Zabalinsiedlung 27.– L.E. Die aussortierten Materialien erbringen täglich ungefähr 2.– L.E., wenn wir die von den Händlern bezahlten Preise von Ende 1983 zu Grunde legen. Die Preise für das Material unterliegen ständigen Schwankungen. In der Zeriba ist zu wenig Platz, um über einen längeren Zeitraum zu sammeln und erst dann zu verkaufen, wenn der Preis gut ist. Die Familien müssen ständig geringe Mengen an den Kleinhändler veräußern und den jeweiligen Preis akzeptieren.

Bei einer bekannten Familie wurde dieses Problem anders gelöst. Sie hatte erst vor kurzem eine eigene Zeriba aufgebaut und besaß noch keine eigenen Schweine, sondern arbeitete für fremde Betriebe. Der tägliche Wasserbedarf der Familie war somit wesentlich geringer und wurde von den Nachbarn gekauft. Diese konnten damit noch ein kleines Extrageschäft machen.

Wasser ist eine wertvolle Ware, und die Frauen haben besondere Techniken zum sparsamen Umgang und zur optimalen Ausnutzung der Recourcen entwickelt. So wird jedes benutzte Wasser zu den Schweinen gekippt. Diese scheinen derart widerstandsfähig zu sein, daß ihnen selbst Seifenwasser nichts ausmacht.

Je älter die Kinder werden, desto stärker werden sie in die Familienarbeit miteinbezogen. Wie überall in Ägypten sind es besonders die jungen Mädchen und die Frauen, die die meiste und schwerste Arbeit zu verrichten haben. Mit Beginn der Pubertät ist es den Mädchen verboten, weiterhin auf den Mülltouren mitzufahren; ihr Arbeits- und Lebensbereich liegt von diesem Zeitpunkt an im Hause. Das Heiratsalter liegt zwischen fünfzehn und siebzehn Jahren, doch muß man davon ausgehen, daß die Mädchen in Wirklichkeit oft jünger sind, und daß oft nur dem koptischen Priester zuliebe das Lebensalter heraufgemogelt wird, um von ihm die Einwilligung zur Ehe zu bekommen. Die jungen Frauen ziehen dann zu den Familien ihrer Ehemänner.

Hier erwarten sie vielfältige Aufgaben. Außer dem täglichen Sortieren der Karrenladung und der Versorgung der Tiere verrichtet die junge Ehefrau – in der Hierarchie der Frauen das schwächste Glied – mit ihren Schwägerinnen, Schwiegermutter und Großmutter die schwere und mühselige Hausarbeit. Neben Wäschewaschen, Brotbacken und Kochen muß sie zum Einkaufen bis in die nächste Siedlung gehen, da die Geschäfte in Mokattam aufgrund ihrer Monopolstellung überteuert sind. Auch gibt es keinen Kooperativladen, der die einzige Möglichkeit für die arme Bevölkerung darstellt, Fleisch, Gemüse und andere Lebensmittel zu erschwinglichen Preisen zu bekommen.

Meist ist der Beginn einer Ehe zugleich der Beginn vieler Schwanger-schaften.

Viele Kinder bedeuten Arbeitsentlastung und Sicherheit. Je mehr Kinder eine Frau hat, desto größer ist die moralische Verpflichtung des Mannes, Frau und Kinder nicht zu verlassen, und für beide ist die Versorgung im Alter sicherer. Da Empfängnisverhütung abgelehnt wird, besteht der Preis dessen in bis zu zwölf Schwangerschaften während eines Lebens. Hierbei gibt es in Mokattam keinerlei medizinische Versorgung; bei den Geburten ist nicht einmal eine Hebamme anwesend, sondern nur die vielerfahrenen Geschlechtsgenossinnen helfen. Mit zunehmendem Alter stellt jede weitere Schwangerschaft eine noch größere Gefährdung für Mutter und Kind dar, diese Situation schlägt sich in der erschreckend hohen Rate der Kindersterblichkeit nieder.

Bei den alten Frauen fällt auf, wie müde und ausgezehrt sie aussehen. Sie ziehen sich von der täglichen Hausarbeit zurück. Ihnen ist es gestattet, sich auszuruhen und so verbringen sie ihren Lebensabend eingebettet und unterstützt von ihrer großen Familie. Die jüngeren erweisen ihnen Respekt und Hochachtung, schätzen ihre Lebenserfahrung und Weisheit.

Der Aufgabenbereich von Mann und Frau sieht sehr unterschiedlich aus. Während die Frauen im häuslichen Bereich arbeiten, pflegen die Männer die Beziehungen zur Außenwelt. Die Familienoberhäupter verwalten die Ökonomie der Zeriba. Sie verkaufen die Schweine und kassieren das Geld vom Händler der Siedlung: kurz, sie tragen die Verantwortung und nehmen innerhalb der Familie ihre patriarchale Machtstellung wahr.*

Einen großen Teil des Tages verbringen die Männer außer Haus, z.B. in einem der vielen Teehäuser, denn dort finden bei Wasserpfeife und süßem Tee die Verkaufsgespräche statt. Die Väter führen ihre

* Die Ertragsrechnung eines mittleren Zabalinbetriebes sieht etwa so aus: (vgl. umseitige Tabelle)

Söhne in die zukünftigen Arbeitsbereiche ein. Sie lernen das Verhandeln mit den Wahis über profitablere Routen und die Verringerung der monatlichen Abzahlungen, sie üben sich in der Kunst des Feilschens und Handelns mit den verschiedenen Materialienhändlern und den Schweineaufkäufern. Die Söhne sind zuständig für die anfallenden Reparaturarbeiten an Eselskarren und Zeriba.

Das durchschnittliche Heiratsalter der Männer liegt zwischen achtzehn und zweiundzwanzig Jahren. Die Vermählung des Sohnes ist für die Familie oft mit einer großen Schwierigkeit verbunden: es fehlt an Wohnraum, denn es gehört sich, daß ein verheiratetes Paar einen eigenen Wohnraum besitzt. Falls eine Zeriba nicht genügend Schlafräume aufweist, wird entweder, soweit es Fundament und Finanzen erlauben, aufgestockt oder vom Hof wird eine 3-mal-3-m-Ecke durch Bretterwände abgeteilt oder der elterliche Schlafraum wird aufgeteilt . . .
Der verheiratete junge Mann lebt so lange in Abhängigkeit zur elterlichen Zeriba, bis es die familiären Finanzen erlauben, daß er sich

	Einnahmen	Ausgaben
Einnahmen aus dem Verkauf von Altmaterial	1,90 L.E.	
Einnahmen aus dem Verkauf der Schweine	2,90 L.E.	
Kapitalkosten		0,45 L.E.
Futter		0,80 L.E.
Gülle und Mistabfuhr		0,10 L.E.
Reparatur- und Wartungskosten		0,30 L.E.
Wahigebühr		0,10 L.E.
Wasser		0,20 L.E.
Summe	4,80 L.E.	1,95 L.E.

Nettogewinn: 2,85 L.E. pro Tag = 85.– L.E. pro Monat

Die Zabalinfamilie liegt mit ihrem Einkommen von umgerechnet ca. 225,– DM im unteren Bereich der Einkommenspyramide. Diese Summe steht dem Betrieb auch nur dann zur Verfügung, wenn alles ohne große Probleme funktioniert. Krankheit, Verletzungen, Seuchen und Tiere, fallende Preise, finanzieller Druck der Behörden können Familien in große finanzielle Probleme stürzen.
Ein Vergleich: das durchschnittliche Monatseinkommen eines Beamten betrug 1984 55 L.E. Dieser kann von seinem Gehalt kaum sich selber, geschweige denn eine Familie ernähren und ist auf Zusatzverdienste angewiesen. Das Schicksal der vielen kleinen Extraverdienste als Voraussetzung zum Überleben teilt er mit dem Großteil der Bevölkerung Cairos. Besser geht es den Handwerkern und Fabrikarbeitern: sie bekommen 200–300 L.E. im Monat.

selbständig macht. Dies ist möglich mit einer Investitionshilfe des Familienoberhauptes, die dann im Laufe der Jahre zu den unterschiedlichsten Bedingungen abzuzahlen ist: sei es, daß der Sohn einen Teil seines erwirtschafteten Profits abzugeben hat, sei es, daß er oder seine Familie weitere Arbeitsleistungen auf der väterlichen Zeriba zu verrichten haben. Diese Form der Starthilfe für neue Zeribas wird auch im weiteren familiären bzw. freundschaftlichen Rahmen praktiziert.*

Abgesehen von einigen Familien, die es zu beachtlichem Besitz gebracht haben, bestehen in der Regel keine höheren Investitionen in großer Anzahl und somit auch keine Kapitalanhäufung. Es heißt, daß gerade bei familiärer Investitionshilfe die Zahlungsbedingungen nicht sehr strikt gehandhabt werden. Die Absprachen über gegenseitige Unterstützung und deren Dauer werden nicht vertraglich festgehalten, sondern finden unter Beisein von älteren Männern und anerkannten Vertrauenspersonen der Siedlung statt. Diese werden auch dann wieder gerufen, wenn das Abhängigkeitsverhältnis aufgelöst wird. Ein solcher 'Rat der Ältesten' wird auch in anderen Konfliktfällen, z. B. bei Familienstreitigkeiten angerufen. Nach traditionellem Ritual und Anhörung beider Parteien fällt er dann sein für alle bindendes Urteil.

Die ältere Generation, die einen Teil ihres Lebens noch in dörflichen Strukturen verbrachte, ist Wahrer der überlieferten Familienstrukturen und Traditionen auch in Mokattam. Sie hat das Geschäft mit dem Müll aufgebaut und verfügt über einen großen Erfahrungsschatz. Die neuen Generationen, schon in Cairo geboren, erfahren die Bindungen an die ursprüngliche Heimat nur noch vermittelt, denn sie wachsen als Kinder einer Cairoer Stadtrandsiedlung auf. Wie mit Konflikten, die aus dieser Situation entstehen können, konkret umgegangen wird, können wir schlecht beurteilen. Aber es sind uns einige

---

* Stehen größere Anschaffungen, wie z. B. die Schaffung von Wohnraum für verheiratete Kinder, ein neuer Esel, Ausbesserungen am Haus oder der Erwerb einer besseren Route an, so wenden sich die Zabalin meist an die Moalems, die Händler der Siedlung, und bekommen dort die nötigen Kredite. Die Zusammenarbeit der Zabalin mit den Moalems scheint besser zu funktionieren als die mit den Wahis. Die Beziehung zu den Wahis ist eine abhängige; der Moalem ist ein gleichberechtigter Geschäftspartner, an den der Zabalin nicht auf Lebzeiten gebunden ist. Außerdem leben Zabalin und Moalems zusammen in der Siedlung.

Fälle bekannt geworden, wo es – was sonst selten war – zum Bruch zwischen Familienoberhäuptern und Söhnen gekommen ist.

Bildung

Die Analphabetenrate in der Siedlung ist hoch, und es sind nach wie vor die Frauen, die bei dem sowieso schon geringen Bildungsangebot keine Chance haben. Bei den erwachsenen Frauen, die ihre Kindheit noch in einem oberägyptischen Dorf verbrachten, sind es gerade zwei bis drei Prozent, die lesen und schreiben gelernt haben. Gemessen an den zukünftig erwarteten Lebensaufgaben von Männern und Frauen, kann man nachvollziehen, daß die Vergabe eines Schulplatzes für die Kinder einer Familie häufig auf die Söhne fällt. Das schlägt sich auch in den statistischen Angaben nieder: vierundzwanzig Prozent aller Haushaltsvorstände können lesen und schreiben. Ebenfalls hoch vertreten ist die Gruppe der älteren Männer, die während ihrer Kindheit in der Gegend um Assiut die Möglichkeit hatten, eine Missionsschule zu besuchen. Diese Männer sind es, die jetzt in der Siedlung eine wichtige Funktion übernehmen: sie sind die Vermittler einer anderen Welt, Übersetzer einer Sprache, die den Zabalin fremd ist und deren Regeln sie nicht beherrschen. Sie sind die Schreiber, die gegen ein Entgelt helfen, Formulare auszufüllen und Briefe zu schreiben.

Heute wie damals scheitert der Schulbesuch der Kinder oft schon an den bürokratischen Voraussetzungen. Zur Anmeldung des Kindes an einer öffentlichen Schule wird eine Geburtsurkunde benötigt. Für wichtige Papiere gibt es in der Zeriba jedoch keinen Aufbewahrungsort und besonders in den Zeiten der ständigen Evakuierungen sind viele Formulare verlorengegangen, oder der Vater hatte es seinerzeit nach der Geburt des Kindes versäumt, eine Urkunde zu beantragen. Diese Kinder, die offiziell gar nicht existieren, werden ihr Leben lang durch die Maschen des staatlichen Netzes fallen – was für sie zumindest den einen Vorteil hat, daß sie nicht zum Militärdienst eingezogen werden können.
Diejenigen, die eine Urkunde besitzen, haben die Möglichkeit, die Grundschule in der nächsten Siedlung zu besuchen. Der Schulweg ist sehr lang; ein Grund, der viele Eltern davon abhält, den Mädchen die Teilnahme zu erlauben.

Im Jahr 1980 richtete die koptische Kirche in Mokattam eine Grundschule ein. Bisher hat sie Platz für nicht mehr als neunzig Schüler. Die Nachfrage ist jedoch weit größer, und leider kann ihr die Kirche nicht mit dem Angebot an Lehrern und Klassen entsprechen. Die Eltern sind am Schulaufbau sehr interessiert. Sie bezahlen die unterrichtenden Lehrer direkt. Familien, die auch sonst einen intensiveren Kontakt zur kirchlichen Sozialarbeit haben, werden am ehesten bei der Aufnahme neuer Schüler berücksichtigt.

Was seitens der Familien gegen den Schulbesuch der Kinder steht, ist häufig nur die Notwendigkeit der täglichen Arbeit. Aber was heißt da: nur!? In diesem Fall sahen wir, daß die Familien unterschiedliche Regelungen treffen: meistens gehören zur Familie viele Kinder im arbeitsfähigen Alter (von vier bis vierzehn Jahren); die wechseln sich während der Woche bei den täglichen Mülltouren ab. Aber wir konnten auch feststellen, daß Eltern entschieden, welchem Kind das Privileg des Schulbesuches zugesprochen wurde. Wie schon erwähnt, fiel dann die Wahl in der Regel auf einen Sohn.

Eine katholische Nonne, Sr. Emanuelle, arbeitet bereits seit sehr langer Zeit mit der koptischen Kirche zusammen und setzt sich in aufopferungswürdiger Weise für die unterschiedlichen (Bildungs-) Belange der Zabalin ein. Neuerdings entwickelt sich ein von ihr initiiertes Gesundheitsprojekt mit besonderem Augenmerk auf gynäkologische Aufgaben sehr positiv.

Zu Beginn der siebziger Jahre hatte Sr. Emanuelle auf einer Müllsiedlung im Nordosten damit angefangen, Nähwerkstätten für die Frauen aufzubauen. In Kursen lernen sie, ihre eigene Kleidung herzustellen sowie gefundene Kleidungsstücke für sich oder die Familie zu verändern. Aus diesen Kursen gehen wiederum Frauen hervor, die, neben der täglichen Arbeit in der Zeriba, weitere Nähkurse leiten oder in den Nähwerkstätten Aufträge für Dritte übernehmen. Ganz nebenbei, wie Emanuelle betont, haben die Frauen außer zuschneiden und nähen auch noch lesen und schreiben gelernt.

Die Kurse verfolgen das Ziel, die Frauen, schwächstes Glied in der Gemeinschaft, auf denen die meiste Arbeit lastet, zu unterstützen und zu stärken und ihnen die Möglichkeit eines 'zusätzlichen Ein kommens' zu verschaffen. Inzwischen sind aus den ehemals kleinen Werkstätten mit ein paar Maschinen richtige Nähschulen geworden, die von Frauen aus der Siedlung selbständig getragen werden.*

* Auch in Moitamedea, einer Müllsiedlung im Westen, waren Nähkurse der Beginn weiterführender Aktivitäten. Dort wurde vor kurzem von Schwester Maria, einer deutschen Nonne, eine Selbsthilfeprojekt initiiert: Mit Spendengeldern aus Deutschland konnten Teile des Bodens gekauft werden, auf dem sich die Müllsiedlung befindet. Eine mögliche Evakuierung der Siedlung stellte nach wie vor die größte Verunsicherung für die Zabalin dar. Nun werden in Eigenarbeit Zeribas aus Stein gebaut. Sechzig Familien haben sich verpflichtet, für die Dauer von drei Jahren täglich ein paar Stunden an den neuen Steinhäusern zu bauen, bis alle beteiligten Familien ihr eigenes Haus haben.

Fotografien
gegliedert nach Tagesablauf und Arbeitsprozessen

مستشفى بروك لعلاج الحيوان

ERECTED BY
BROOKE HOSPITAL
FOR ANIMALS
1980

Anno Wilms, geboren in Berlin, fotografische Ausbildung in Hamburg und Berlin. Als freiberufliche Fotografin international tätig für Ausstellungen, Bildbände, Zeitschriften und Werbung.

Eigene Bildbände:

Berlin – Impressionen einer Stadt (1970)
Zigeuner (1972)
Bummel durch Berlin (1974)
Berlin (1977)
Transvestiten (1978)
Israel (1981)
Rastafari (1982)
Ägypten (1982)
Beduinen (1985)

Ausstellungen:

Bilder aus aller Welt (1963)
Freie Berliner Kunstausstellung (1971, 1972, 1973)
Foto de Arte Contemporaneo Mexico City und San Francisco (1980)
Kunstverein München (1982)

Product Development in Glass Structures

D1674245

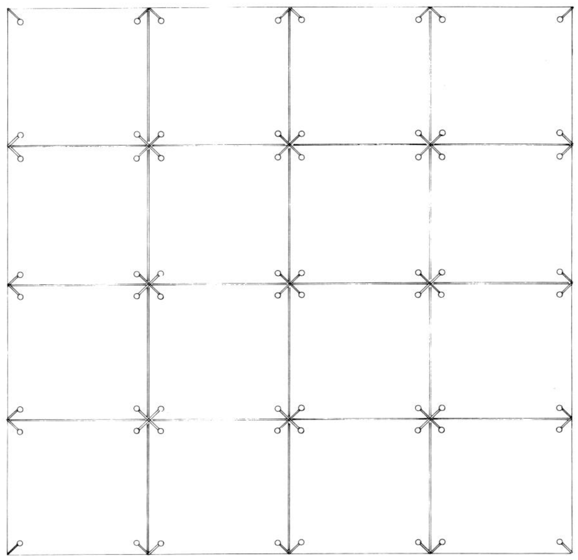

MICK EEKHOUT

Product Development in Glass Structures

Uitgeverij 010 Publishers, Rotterdam

Copyright 1990 Mick Eekhout / Uitgeverij 010 Publishers

CIP-GEGEVENS KONINKLIJKE BIBLIOTHEEK, DEN HAAG

Eekhout, Mick

Product Development in Glass Structures / Mick Eekhout. –
Rotterdam : Uitgeverij 010 Publishers. – Ill.
ISBN 90-6450-111-4
SISO 694.9 UDC 691.6:72 NUGI 923
Trefw.: glasconstructies ; bouwkunst.

Design by Rudo Hartman / Den Haag

Photographs by
Annet Borchert 46
Theo Buijsse 70, 71
Fred van Dijken 26, 27
Klats page 43
Paul Pelene 47
Chris Pennarts page 8, 9, 22, 23 and 71
Van der Vlugt & Claus cover photograph, page 21, 52, 54, 55,
58, 60 and 61
Sybolt Voeten 28

Printed by Tulp bv / Zwolle

Foreword

Only a very few architects and engineers experience the direct synergetic relationship of design and production with the benefit of continuous feedback between intentions and realizations. Mick Eekhout is one of that rare breed following in the footsteps of Eiffel, Brunel, Behrens, Prouvé and others. It may be no accident that he once worked with Renzo Piano and Frei Otto.

In his unusual role of architect, engineer, product designer and manufacturer he has been able to translate his dreams of new forms of construction into the reality of building in many parts of the world. Since our first meeting at the Lightweight Structures in Architecture Conference in Australia in 1986 our paths have crossed many times. Firstly in our interests in long span structures and space frames, then in the use of fabric structures and more recently in exciting possibilities of lightness and transparency involving new ways of using glass. Our own work at East Croydon Station which is historically parallel to Mick Eekhout's own investigations into toughened glass, has led to a continued dialogue between us on the methods of supporting large spanning glazed structures.

We are in agreement that the technology involved in the use of glass, glazing systems and curtain walling is advancing rapidly, in many cases outstripping the knowledge generally available within the design professions and the industry. This book, with its theoretic background and examples of practice, including the innovative use of glass at the Glass Music Hall in Amsterdam could, therefore, not have come at a more opportune time as a continuation of existing knowledge.

It is a credit to Mick Eekhout's energy and resource that he has been able to summarize the latest production techniques and theories and also to demonstrate his own many examples of their use. The book thus presents the possibility of glass not only as an infill within a glazing system but also as a structural material in its own right. As such it is an invaluable statement of the state of the art of glazing and its method of support and will be a source book for those intending to extend the existing possibilities of these new technologies in the future.

Alan J. Brookes PhD B Arch
Alan Brookes Associates, London

Contents

Theory

Practice

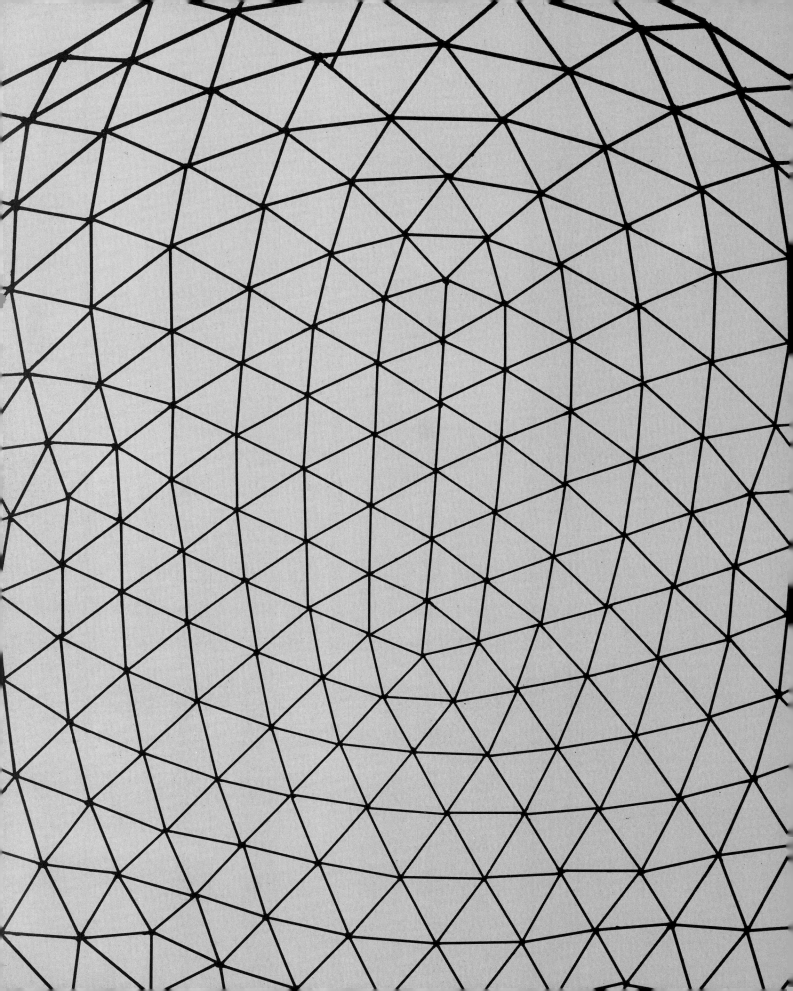

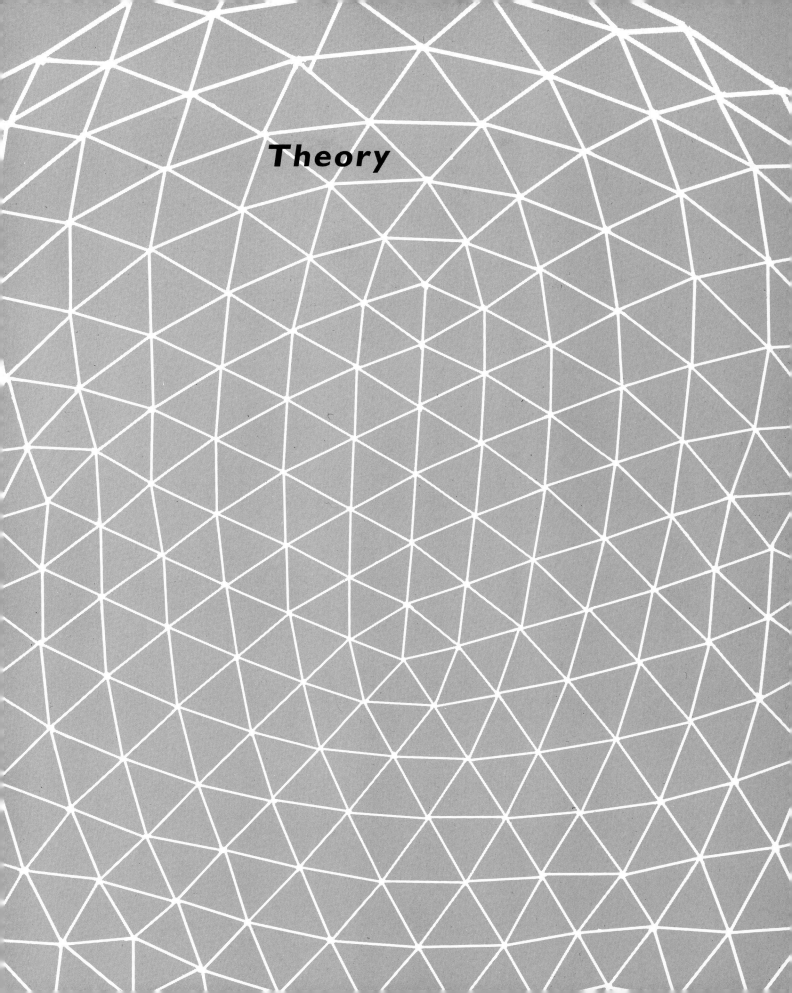

Theory

1 The Galleria Vittorio Emmanuele II, designed by architect Mengoni, marks the zenith of the development of the arcade building type, and is both space and building. Built in 1865—1867 just after the unification of Italy by an English turnkey builder. Diameter octagonal dome 36.6 m summit height dome 41,8 m, vault width 14.5 m height 29.3 m. Longitudional wing 196.6 m, lateral wing 105.1 m.

1   The Importance of Glass in Architecture

Artificial glass has fascinated people ever since the discovery through oven processing, in general taken as around 3000 BC in the Near East. Around 1500 BC transparent glass was developed in Egypt, and the invention of the glass blowpipe in Syria in the 2nd century BC was another major step in early glass technology. In ancient times glass was used in small items of artificial jewellery, tools for household purposes and primitive chemistry. The transparency of glass, a product of 3/4 sand (silicium dioxide), chalk (calcium carbonate for better weather resistance) and soda (natrium carbonate for lowering the melting point), has always been strongly connected with its perception in daylight and artificial light. Its transparency and reflectiveness made it a unique material for a very long time. The flattening of blown curved glass surfaces into small glass plates was gratefully adopted in mediaeval architecture to close openings with leaded glass in the walls of buildings. Coloured or stained glass played an even more sophisticated role in the sunlight-washed windows of Gothic architecture and was greatly used as an architectural phenomenon of filtering coloured daylight. With the production techniques of the industrial revolution flat glass plates became larger in size, stimulating the building industry to erect glass houses as a new architectural archetype in the 19th century (fig 1). The best-known example was the Crystal Palace built for the first time in Hyde Park, London, for the World Exposition of 1851, rebuilt in Sydenham in 1854 and burned down in 1936. In this building some 80,000 m2 of glass panels were used, a gigantic quantity, even in that mid-Victorian period of industrial revolution. The Crystal Palace was a well-publicized product of the era; a product of what we would nowadays call mechanization, mass production, prefabrication, standardization, modular construction, integration of construction / services / sun shading, rapid site assembly, critical path organization and a great deal of ingenuity. In its day the Crystal Palace accelerated a glass mania for similar buildings all over Europe, and a large number of exhibition buildings, glass arcades, market coverings and winter gardens were built after 1851. With the ingenuity of the engineers of the industrial revolution climatic control by ventilation, heating and sunshading were solved on an equally adequate level.

But the position of the individual glass plates in rigid putty and with wooden mullions on cast-iron substructures proved to pose problems of glass breakage, water leakage and structural erosion in the long term. Glass houses in the last century were largely built by wealthy institutions, private owners and building developers, particularly the shop-ping arcades and covered markets. This tendency stopped abruptly during the First World War. Lack of maintenance was one reason (glass roofs had to be replaced every 20 or 30 years), deterioration of materials another, while wartime destruction ended completely the popularity of glass structures on the European continent. Timber mullions proved unable to withstand rainwater, and iron and steel T-sections corroded with equal speed; putty was too rigid and brittle and after some time broke into pieces. Most of the once- famous 19th century glass-covered structures ended up leaking or were burned down.

But the developments in greenhouses for true horticultural purposes went on. In the Netherlands in particular, with the enormous economic pressure from horticulture and agriculture, new generations of greenhouse systems were developed in practice. They are built now in galvanized steel, aluminium and large thin sheets of glass, or polycarbonate sheets. Due to the overwhelming industrialization and standardization in this Dutch building industry, these greenhouses at present still cost not much more than Dfl 50,-/m2, completely watertight, including ventilating windows and concrete foundations. Yet these greenhouses have been optimized for their own horticultural function; insurance companies have to pay for storm and hail damages regularly: thus greenhouse technology cannot be used directly in buildings for people. Adaptations of this greenhouse technology into architecture (for example in housing) have to conform to the more severe international standard codes of practice for the building industry. But at this moment the Dutch greenhouse industry can be described as the most optimized building industry in the Netherlands, with a large export turnover.

Immediately after the First World War, in their hopes for new and better times, visionary architects like Ludwig Mies van der Rohe designed glass-clad highrise office blocks like crystal-clear prisms. These concepts would only be realized thirty years later in a primitive form, and sixty years later in their present definitive form. From then on, glass was seen as a prime transparent space-enveloping material. In the 1960s James Sterling realized a number of university buildings in Oxford, Cambridge and Leicester, England, where roof surfaces of glass in standardized patented mullions played a major role in the design. His projects attracted new attention to large glass roof and wall applications in European architecture. It was only with the further development through improvements in physical properties in the 1970s that tinted glass was seen as a surface with a colour of its own, as an independent building material with much improved material properties. Reflection also became important. The perception of glass became one of a reflecting outside surface for abstractly conceived buildings instead of a transparent membrane as used by the earlier Functionalist architects. So glass was appreciated more and more by architects of the 1980s as an abstracting fascia-building material, especially when mechanical connections were no longer clearly visible, as in structural glass: large exterior glazed planes as a crystal surface, viewed semantically.

Another significant tendency of the period since the 1950s was the product development of glass to improve it in terms of thermal insulation value by bonding double glass panels; and, furthermore, mechanically in terms of strength, against thermal breakage and lately, against vandalism. This led to the intensive use of tempered glass (a process developed in the 1930s) and laminated glass (multiple sheets of glass bonded with PVB foil or epoxy resin). The so-called float glass process was developed by Pilkington (UK) and forms nowadays the basis for regular low-cost and technically reliable glass productions. Chemically toughened glass meant a breakthrough in high-strength thin glass sheets. Borosilicate glass was developed as a technically adequate answer to the demand for fire-resistant glass. (New non-toughened glass types are being developed to this end to be used as a cheaper substitute for borosilicate glass.) The many possibilities generated by the extra strengthening of glass in composite panels led to the concept of real structural glass.

2   What is Structural Glazing?

The description 'Structural Glazing' has a number of different interpretations in building technology, taking their point of departure from the architectural or the structural point of view.

Architectural Meaning of Structural Glazing

In the first place 'structural glazing' is an abbreviation of the term 'structurally sealed glazing', meaning a method of attaching glass panels to the substructure in curtain walling. In the early days of curtain walls it indicated anything other than fixing with screw strips. This change-over from mechanical to sealed connections was heralded by a number of remarkable peaks that created a great impression, and sometimes great confusion too. One of the most memorable cases was the Hancock building in Boston USA, designed in the early seventies by architect I.M.Pei & Partners of New York and nicknamed the 'Plywood Skyscraper'. This design made a deep and confusing impression as an example of structural glazing for curtain walls in its experimental days (fig 2). In

2 The John P. Hancock (insurance) building in Boston USA , photographed in 1973, nicknamed 'the plywood skyskraper'; her too flexible steel skeleton caused numerous glass panels to be sucked out in windy weather. Sailing panels damaged more panels on their way down.

this building many glass panels were sucked out by wind during its completion in 1973, and replaced by plywood panels. After the components, including the rubber gaskets around the glass panels, were tested thoroughly and confirmed to be reliable, the curtain wall was repaired, and so was the confidence in this type of connection. The glass panels were in fact sucked out because of movement by the building as a whole. (This building is now crowned by an anti-balance weight which reduces the movement by windloading of the tall building.) So in the end it was not this early structural glass that was to blame for the building's nickname, but the main steel structure. Nevertheless the picture of the Hancock building in those days is still remembered as a token of experimenting and prototyping in the building industry.

Prototypes

In terms of product responsibility it brought to the attention how narrow the path of new developments can sometimes be: the difference between a successful or a bad product can at times only be discovered afterwards. This 'sword of Damocles' hangs above all new product developments by architects and building component designers. Very generally, however, these cases have led to an extreme cautiousness and the high degree of conservatism prevalent in the glass industry. Broadly speaking this applies equally well to the building industry as a whole. The problem for a whole new generation of young and technically progressive building component designers is 'the prototype'. How to work with new materials, new production techniques and new application systems or static systems and aiming at a new architectural functioning while knowing that the most one will achieve is to realize a 'prototype building'. In those cases clients must be satisfied with the prototype nature of their buildings. Small-scale prototypes are designed, studied and tested in a limited way, but only real prototype buildings will prove ideas to be right or wrong, will prove that there are elements, components or combinations of elements, components and their positions that need improvement. Almost all new buildings suffer from inconveniences because the building industry in general does not offer enough room for a full building component development. Hence 'Technical Architecture' with medium budgets can suffer more because of a lack of time and money to develop the newly designed and arranged technology to perfection. Technical Architecture in general suffers from the large shift of labour from the building site to the engineering office and its consequences: often a mistake has been made in the design and engineering department, and not discovered during production of the individual components. Only site assembly will reveal the mistake, usually at great expense. This can be compared with more traditional building methods, where the minor ailments have been put right through the years. Most architects are not used to develop their designs in a design laboratory, as Renzo Piano does. In normal contracts there is not enough room either for parallel testing at research institutes. This is partly because the fees of the research institutes concerned are very high compared with the value-for-money activities in the building industries; but also because most clients simply do not want to pay the extra amount as a private contribution to the general state of the art. Lastly, the design profession lacks an established mechanism to bundle new knowledge and then disperse it again (see par. 5: Boosting). The omission of technical research and development in the planning stage could very well lead to claims for remuneration afterwards. This, in short, forms the 'sword of Damocles' of prototyping in architectural technology.

The growing tendency among architects to design in an abstract, non-material-bound way has strongly stimulated the use of glass as a cladding material for exterior walls and roofs. This tendency was reinforced shortly after the first oil crisis of 1973 when in European glass industries a search began for glass panels with greatly improved insulating qualities to beat the heightened energy costs of glass-clad buildings. The demand for smooth building surfaces and low maintenance costs led to the application of glass panels structurally sealed to the aluminium substructure with silicone and provided with a silicone watertight seal between the glass panels. These techniques were exploited on a large scale in the USA even before 1973, necessitated by the implications of American highrise building technology, and imported into Europe only later. In fact, even after twenty years of experience in the USA, structurally sealed glass is still not permitted in certain countries, such as West Germany. In those cases the silicone sealing and glueing techniques still must be combined with mechanical screwing techniques that are safely traditional, caused by presumptions as to fire behaviour and long-term failure of structural sealants (see par 12, Transworld Marine Dome). These descriptions all concern curtain walling and skylights. In these cases loadings are only the external ones acting on one glass panel. No further structural loadings are taken. 'Structural' in the architectural sense refers only to the mode of connection to the subframe, i.e. with a sealant. The confusion grows when people commonly refer to any type of architectural cladding in which a sealant is used for watertightness alone as 'structural'.

Structural Meaning of Structural Glazing

Quite different and more interesting scientifically is the line of thought taken by the civil engineering meaning of 'structural glazing'; glass structures that bear external loadings over more than one glass panel and contain bending and normal stresses. The strength properties of heat-strengthened and tempered glass challenge a number of building component designers and engineers such as Marc Malinowski, Peter Rice and the author to see where the limits of suitability lie for glass panels to be used as loadbearing structural elements in structures that contain an absolute but balanced visual minimum of metal components. This book explains the quest by the author for such structures and his development process of glass panels from non-structural, via half-structural to the current state of the art of a fully structural use, in the structural engineering sense. The ultimate goal and ideal of this quest is to build horizontal roof structures where glass panels carry normal stresses and form the greater part of the total structure, while a visual minimum amount of metal components play their complementary role in the structural entity. From an architectural angle the art will be to attain a harmony of transparent planes and scaling metal elements. Too transparent has no architectural meaning either.

This goal has been set as an ultimate objective, knowing that even after a long period of experimentation it might prove to be 'one bridge too far'. Or maybe even during the course of this quest for glass structures another glass or glass-like material must first be invented and developed, one that does not suffer from brittleness or other negative properties (as Professor Dick Dicke hinted at during the examination for the author's doctoral degree on May 23, 1989).

In particular the book describes those cases of an ever-increasing degree of experimentation and difficulty carried out by the company of Octatube Space Structures bv in Delft, Netherlands during the last few years. The state of the art is June 1990. The process of Design + Research + Development + Application of real structural glass is described from the wider viewpoint of the author as a product-architect combining the skills of an architect, a structural designer and an industrial designer, stimulated by the possibilities and responsibilities of the specialist-producer.

3 The Product-Architect

In the Netherlands the term 'product-architect' has been known since November 18, 1988 when the author proposed it at the first 'Booosting' congress in Rotterdam (see par 5). For him, the role of the product-architect is to design, research and develop building components independent of the actual design of buildings, and to apply these building components in the overall design of buildings normally designed by independent project-architects (his clients).

The product-architect emphasizes the potential of new materials (Material Science), production techniques (Material Processing) and application systems (Structural Engineering and Architecture) and combines it with the analytical approach of the industrial designer and the know-how of on-site building techniques belonging to the architect, plus the creativity of both professions. So the field of action and also the abilities of the product-architect combine those of the architect, the industrial designer and, in this case, the structural engineer. Figure 3 gives an Organogram of a typical design and development process for building products and components (*Architecture in Space Structures*). This scheme is the result of analyses by the author of several product development processes. It has the advantage of visual communication for designers, so it requires only a brief comment:

- Phase 1: Orientation and product concept showing a preliminary design phase with provisory market evaluation.
- Phase 2: Testing market on design concept showing the market research on the first product concepts.
- Phase 3: Techniques and costs of prototypes showing the necessary mainly technical in-house developments to complete the prototype.
- Phase 4: Prototype and market showing the confrontation in the market with the developed prototype and its evaluation.
- Phase 5: Launching of a product showing the process of production of the first application, with evaluation for duplication and further standard production.

It is the author's opinion that more new materials and building components could benefit from the ability of the integrated approach of the product-architect to lift out components, to ennoble them and to reapply them in architecture (i.e. buildings designed by independent project architects). These components could range from skeleton structures in reinforced concrete or metal, wall panels in concrete, steel, aluminium, plastics, wood or glass, interior partitioning walls, stairs, climate control installations and other infrastructure, etc, and combinations of components. A great number of building components merit sophistication in a functional, technical, material, aesthetic and financial sense.

In the world of young Dutch architects some further definitions are used to describe similar or connected activities:
- 'Archineer', introduced by Jan Westra in 1985, indicates activities in the field of projects and products done by one person – an integrated approach. The international pioneers are Renzo Piano and the British High-Tech family of Norman Foster, Richard Rogers, Nicholas Grimshaw, Tony Farell, Richard Hordon, Alan Brookes and the like. As a rule their most impressive buildings are masterpieces of as much overall design as innovative component detailing, but almost no spin-off as a result of their efforts has been accepted within the normal building industry. High-Tech is for the few, to be gazed at in wonder. The Dutch 'archineers' generally have to cope with less sophisticated buildings for clients with smaller budgets. They operate in the Middle-Tech market but usually in connection with the normal building industry. The difference between an archineer and a product-architect is that the product-architect does not design complete buildings, only building components. The archineer does both.
- 'Industrial Architect' introduced by Jan Pesman of Cepezed of Delft NL in 1984 covers the same aspects as the 'archineer', with slightly more emphasis on that of industrialization, designing both entire buildings and its building components.

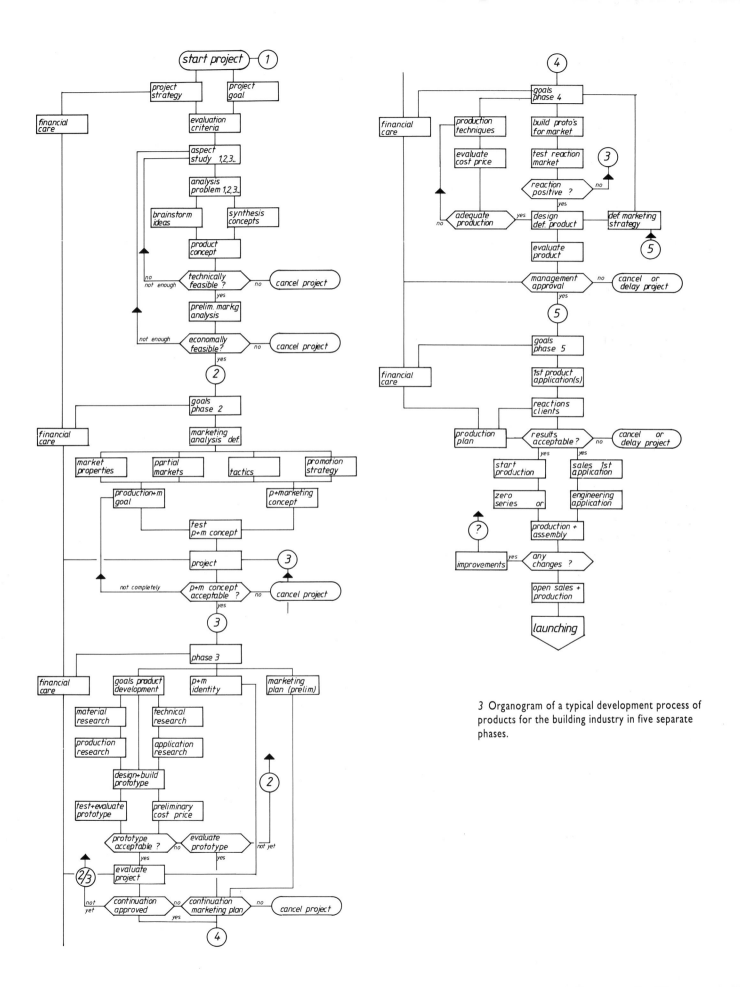

3 Organogram of a typical development process of products for the building industry in five separate phases.

• 'Building Component Designer' is the term preferred by the BNA (Association of Dutch Architects). This is in order not to waste the term 'architect' which after a long struggle finally has been given legal status by Dutch Parliament, and also not to confuse them with project architects assigned within one architectural practice under a senior partner to a certain project; having the term (overall) project architect, as opposed to product-architect.

In comparison, in the author's opinion, the 'product-architect' sets out to give his products a certain 'extra value' with respect to design suited to architecture of the same level, and elevates it from being 'just a building component'. A product-architect aspires to making products for the building industry with a higher aesthetic quality, as does the interior designer in his professional area, often within the limits of the overall design of the project-architect. Without this architectural objective building component design can be a very boring affair for an educated architect, as the results seem only to be appreciated by contractors in terms of money and delivery time. This book has been written from the point of view of a product-architect.

4 Designing, Experimenting and Building

What is the status of the product-architect? He could have an independent office for building component design and development (like an industrial designer). Alternatively, Building Component Development could be one of the departments of his architect's office. Also he could have a firm relationship through a separate long running contract with one or more producers, he might even be employed by a producer in a product-development department in a production company. His activities can be restricted to design, or he can have a development laboratory or even a production facility for 'O' series. He can be involved in initial Design, Research and Development of a new building component and sometimes he is also engaged to launch Application Engineering of his product into the designs of other project architects. These are various options for the building component designer or product-architect, which will be fulfilled each time according to personal abilities, technical capacities and commercial possibilities. It is because of the advantage of the product-architect's know-how that he could in fact be employed in all the forementioned situations.

At all events, the position of the producent-architect is usually as well focused on production (Design, Research and Development) as on consumption (Applications). Depending on his relationship with the producer, the large range of sub-sequent applications every specialist-producer normally works on enables him to design a building component product and bring it to maturity within a comparatively short time. And this without the danger of developments ceasing after the completion of only one prototype building, as there will be subsequent projects. The project architect's office is wary of halting a development when one major client terminates a project or when a project has been completed. And very often architects feel that secrets have to be kept in the office to prevent colleagues from taking advantage without paying or at least investing the same energy on an equal basis. This of course leads to the invention of the wheel over and over again. It is nothing new that knowledge fades when the older generation is succeeded by a younger one, but do we have to start all over again every time in one generation? Production orientation means more continuity in product development. This connection with production results in literal information and figurative inspiration from materials and production techniques in a more physical way. In the Netherlands the market for independent building component designers and product-architects' offices is growing steadily, as it is recognized as a new phenomenon with potential. A crucial element is the availability of a laboratory where in larger companies longer-running product developments can take place, while in smaller companies guided by small experimental 'develop-and-build' contracts, a less costly but slower and less far-reaching step-by-step method of development can be maintained. The process described in this book is a result of a slow step-by-step process (sometimes interrupted by too many standard projects). The 'feel' of materials and their physical presence have always been the source of know-how for any specialist, and has proved very inspiring to all manner of material-orientated designers. New opportunities begin and end with materials and production processes. Furthermore, the real building opportunities of a number of successive applications of building components in different buildings enable continuous feedback and product improvement from every initial product design up to the launching of the matured building component product.

5 Boooosting

Different countries in Europe have adopted the tendency described above in different ways. In England High-Tech architects treat the development of total architectural schemes and the individual building components simultaneously. In Italy most product development for the producers in the building industry is done by professional architects. In the Netherlands the need was felt to stimulate the production of building components with a shot of creativity by architectural designers and a boost in new materials and production techniques by industrial designers. The desire to reinforce the mutual cooperation of architectural with industrial (and sometimes structural) design on the one hand and production on the other, led in the Netherlands in 1988 to the formation of a foundation called 'Booosting'. In English, the aim is clearly to stimulate these combined developments; in Dutch the three O's stand for the unity of: 'Ontwerpen', 'Onderzoeken' and 'Ontwikkelen' ('Design', 'Research' and 'Development'). The foundation has its office in The Hague and is to exist for three years. It is hoped that by then this stimulating initiative will have been accepted by a more eager design and development attitude in Dutch producing companies and that education of building component designers and product-architects will have been institutionalized in academic circles. The author was one of the founders of Booosting, but conversely the Booosting programme did much to stimulate the development of the quest for glass space structures described in this book. Without Booosting this quest would not have developed so clearly.

The main goal of Booosting is 'to stimulate Design, Development, Research and Application of industrial building products and building components so as to heighten the quality of the built environment'.

This goal will be reached by:
• Stimulation of contact between architects, industrial designers, advisors and producers of building products and components;
• Publication of the results of this design, development, research and application for professional clients, government, fellow architects, industrial designers, advisors, producers and contractors;
• Publication of the acquired know-how for the schools for architects, technical engineers and industrial designers to confront students with the importance of material applications, production and building methods, and to increase their level of knowledge.

The activities of Booosting include:
• Initiating product development teams from parties of different disciplines, with the aim of developing products with 'extra value';
• Exhibitions showing the results of these developments;
• Presentation Meetings at which the producing company's philosophy and strategy are discussed;
• Product Quality Meetings at which designers, researchers and producers of building products discuss practical problems before, during and after their application in practice;
• Compilation of brochures, lectures, articles and books on the subject to spread the word to a larger audience. The first

Booosting book is entitled *Tussen Traditie en Experiment*, edited by Jan Westra (Rotterdam 1990).

Booosting hopes that the new developed building products and components will thus acquire an extra value that can be described as follows:
1 Synergetic result of cooperating parties
2 Stimulating O+O+O (Design, R & D)
3 Challenging innovation
4 Industrial production
5 Original and new initiative
6 Potential market value
7 Solution for standard objectives/applications
8 Stimulating creative solution

Among the first products are a 2.5 m high mini-media unit of 100 x 150 mm to fit within the constructional elements of a house for the electronic measurement of gas, water and telephone/electricity supplies designed by industrial designer Marcel Vroom and architect Victor Mani together with the producers Holec, Schlumberger, PTT and utility boards. This design will need some years of development processing because of the involvement of many parties and the generality of its application. Architects and critics see it as a real 'bombshell' in housing design.

Another design for polycarbonate wall cladding elements for social housing has been designed by architect Jan Brouwer, industrial designer Jaap Koning and polycarbonate producer General Electric. Architects' office Cepezed, industrial designer Bas Pruyser and interior furniture producer Ahrend are completing a design for integrated office furniture and infrastructure.

6 Material Properties

For an architecturally trained designer like the author, the numerical side of the Science of Materials is not the most compelling aspect of the profession. Yet the relative large differences in properties of the different building materials provide a reasonable indication of whether combinations of these materials are desirable or possible. Just by comparing these properties some basic and very logical conclusions can be drawn. Scientists generally go very deep, but hardly ever step over the borders of their own specialist territory, while architects have to be aware of all the principles involved.

Young's Modulus of Elasticity

Approximate E-values in N/mm2 are:
• Steel 210,000
• Aluminium 67,000 to 73,000

- Ordinary glass 73,000 to 75,000
- Tempered glass 73,000 to 75,000
- Borosilicate glass 63,000
- PMMA 3,200
- PC 2,300
- Wood 14,000

Of all transparent building materials glass is the best suited for structural purposes. Both polycarbonate (PC) and acrylate (PMMA) have a far less favourable modulus of elasticity (2,300 / 3,200 N/mm2 compared with 75,000 N/mm2 for normal and tempered glass), meaning that the rigidity of these materials is far less; thus deflections under external loadings applied to PMMA and PC are much larger.

Tensile Strength

The maximum tensile strengths in N/mm2 of the different building materials are:
- Mild Steel 360
- Alu alloy AlMgSi 0.5 215
- Ordinary glass 40
- Tempered glass 200
- Borosilicate glass 100
- PMMA 70 to 110
- PC 60 to 100
- Wood 100

The maximum tensile strength of glass is 40 N/mm2, but that of tempered glass is as much as 200 N/mm2, while that of PC is 60 to 100 and PMMA 70 to 110. More noticeable is that the maximum compressive strength of all glasses is 800 to 1000 N/mm2 (without the influences of buckling).

Brittleness

The most deviant property of glass applied as an element of a primary structure, compared with other structural materials, is its brittleness, which turns out to be most decisive for the use of glass as a structural material. The 'Achilles' heel', the weakness of glass (and to a far lesser extent some cast metals such as certain aluminium alloys), is caused by this brittleness. Glass has no capacity to re-distribute high tensions. Small stress concentrations and imperfections in the glass surface can cause concentration factors of over 100. Tempered glass is even more sensitive to imperfections in the surface than normal glass, when the sensitive internal stress balance (compression outside, tension inside) gets disturbed.

Very broadly speaking, there are two fracture mechanisms competing to break a material:

- Plastic Flow
- Brittle Cracking.

The material will succumb to whichever mechanism is weaker. If it yields before it cracks, it is ductile. If it cracks before it yields, it is brittle. The potentiality of both forms of failure is always present in most materials. Yielding is a safe and much desired property, spontaneous cracking an undesirable property for a structural material.

Time and Creep

Creep in glass and tempered glass is practically nil, but in PC and PMMA it is fairly high, and figures are known in Material Science. Some glass industries tell us that in time glass will deform (even 'frozen' liquid will flow): hence many old mirrors have become bobbly by now while old window panes are never flat. But data on the time within which this happens is completely absent. Some glazers maintain that old large and thick shop window panes are always difficult to remove because the lower end appears to be thicker than the upper end, and has become wedged in the glass groove. Older glass products are more polluted with salts which is the reason why old glass panels have this tendency to deform in time. The current methods of producing glass eliminate almost all pollutions so that the effect of creep in modern glass panels can be safely disregarded. Another effect of time is that glass suffers from fatigue, when applied under static or dynamic loading. This is due to weathering. Long-term tests have been installed in the Octa Lab to research these effects.

Wood creeps, as we all know from heavily-loaded tiled roofs built of timber beams. Steel does not creep. In using reinforced concrete as a substructure, one should remember that creep in reinforced concrete is generally assumed to stop after two years. This fact can be extremely important for the detailing of glass walls suspended from reinforced concrete beams, as post-adjustment would be required.

Thermal Conductivity

The values for the respective materials are given in W/mK:
- Steel 40-50
- Aluminium 200
- Glass 0.80
- PMMA 0.07 to 0.21
- PC 0.12 to 0.19
- Timber 0.12 to 0.16

Thermal Expansion

Thermal expansion is important for the differences between structural and cladding materials and between cooperating materials in structure or cladding. Values are given in 10.-6 m/mK:
- Steel 12
- Aluminium 24
- Borosilicate glass 3.25
- Glass (other types) 9
- PMMA 70
- PC 65
- Timber 3 to 5

There will be problems when values of cooperating materials differ too much. PMMA and PC expand seven times as much as glass. The combination of steel and glass causes less problems than that of aluminium and glass. In general glass panels fracture often because of hindered thermal expansion, so rubber or elastic cushioning is advisable in the restrained areas.

Specific Gravity

Values in kN/m3:
- Steel 78
- Aluminium 27
- Borosilicate glass 20.5
- Normal / tempered glass 25
- PMMA 12
- PC 12
- Timber 7

Behaviour at High Temperatures

The maximum workable temperature in degrees Celsius:
- Steel 550
- Aluminium 250
- Ordinary glass 60-110
- Tempered glass 270
- Borosilicate glass 800
- PMMA 80
- PC 115

These figures show why fire-resistant panels have to be made of steel and steel-strengthened elements (wire mesh in glass). No ordinary transparent material will have a good fire rating. Only borosilicate glass has a better fire rating (30 up to 120 minutes in special cases), but is much more expensive: Dfl 500,-/m2 compared with Dfl 50,-/m2 for float glass. Sudden temperature differences can lead to stresses twice as large as those caused by a constant temperature loading. Glass is more sensitive to sudden undercooling (tension) than to sudden heating (compression).

Chemical Resistance

Glasses in general have a good chemical resistance: acid resistance is excellent in all sorts of glass, while the alkali resistance of float glass is slightly less than that of tempered glass and borosilicate glass.

7 Production Techniques

Since we are interested in the extent to which glass could be used as a real structural material, the failure mechanism for glass can be seen as follows. Glass is cooled during manufacture so fast that the molecules do not have time to sort themselves out into crystals. So cooled glass is a solidified liquid, not a crystallized solid. However, the tendency to crystallize is present and given time this will happen. This is known as devitrification. It involves shrinkages; the glass is often weakened, and sometimes even falls to pieces during the process. It will always fracture in the same brittle way. In fact, if we want to prevent the glass from cracking we have to subject it to compression. This can be done by heating the glass panels again, and chilling the two outer skins of the hot glass panels during fabrication very quickly, so that the two outer skins form with the core a compression + tension mechanism. When the outer surfaces have cooled they solidify, while the core is still hot (700°C). The shrinking during cooling of the core causes the outer skins to be compressed, while the central core will remain under tension. So the outer skin of this so-called 'tempered' glass is under compression, the core under tension. This is a mechanism to avoid surface cracks, but it hides internal cracks too. The mechanism is the same for nodular iron and cast aluminium: the outer surface can be very smooth, while irregularities can be concealed within the material. Heat-strengthened glass has gone only through half the temperature process. When it breaks, there will be larger fragments than the grit-like particles of shattered tempered glass. In general, the smaller the pieces after breaking, the higher the temperature of the heating process. An advantage is that these heat-strengthened panels are generally flatter because as a rule the temperature process is more controllable (there is less heat input). The former vertical hardening ovens produced glass panels with the characteristic suspension points. In fact because of the free suspension, the glass panels suffered from uncontrollable deformation during cooling, which is no longer the case with today's horizontal rolling ovens. This horizontally heat-treated glass is much flatter, but is generally restricted to a panel size of 2.1 x 4.2 m. All drilling, grinding and other smoothing will be done before the heat treatment.

After strengthening, the final product is a glass panel with higher tensile strengths and a higher impact strength too. Great care has to be taken that the glass surface is not scratched by a sharp tool, because then it will shatter into thousands of small splinters. Try to keep glass panels away from vandals. Or conversely, sharp glass hammers are a safety tool for breaking out of an all-glass cage (as discussed during the design process of the Glass Music Hall in Amsterdam, see par. 16).

In tempered glass panels possible cracks are avoided by the compression mechanism. Consequently, bolt-and-hole type connections can be best achieved using a pretensioning type of bolt connection: in that case the hole edges are not loaded by the bolt on flush, (with the inherent danger of enlarging the micro-cracks around the bolt hole by drilling), but the pretensioned bolt compresses the two outside metal rings or components onto the glass where mutual friction will provide the connection force. The friction force can be heightened by grinding or blasting the surface around the bolt hole (before the hardening process). Alternatively, a flush-type connection will have to contain an intermediate material with 'plastic' behaviour between bolt and glass hole to avoid local top tensions in the hole, from which micro-cracks can lead to serious cracks. Another idea might be to fill in the irregular left-over spaces in the holes between the outsides of the holes and the bolts with liquid epoxy, to arrive at a firm, abrasive connection. This is a technique developed to renovate old nailed railway bridges with slotted bolt holes. In this case the method is a means to isolate metal from glass and to adjust glass panels to the exact size required. The type of connection will be determined by the vulnerability of the irregularity between bolt shaft and bolt hole.

Regarding the scale of the glass panels, a possible compression (normal) force introduces the danger of buckling the panel, so that the largest commercially available panel thicknesses of tempered glass (12, 15 and 19 mm) will have to be used; these are fairly expensive per volume. It would then be preferable – if at all possible – to load the glass panels under tensile (normal) force instead of compression: that is, to suspend rather than stack them. The description 'curtain wall' would then live up to its full literal meaning! Consequently, with roofs it would be better to combine glass panels in the tensile instead of in the compression zone. Another solution to avoid buckling in glass plates with normal stresses is given in paragraph 21 in the 'Concertina-Glass' space frame proposal of the Delft students Rob Bakker and Gerald Lindner.

The thermal hardening process is one of the interesting production techniques of structural glass. It was invented decades ago, but is still the basis of current structural glass types. Another remark has to be made on the installation of glass panels: although tempered glass panels are very strong they are likely to shatter into thousands of small pieces, for instance if not paid adequate and proper attention during hoisting and installation.

8 Structural Systems

The static systems applicable to glass structures will all be based on the use of glass panels. Glass bars do exist but the nature of these fibreglass bars filled with epoxy is not translucent. Moreover the connections are still quite laborious, so in this book glass is considered only in panel-form, and not as bars. The most simple solution is the classical vertical glass panel, able to make a vertical span with or without metal or glass ribs. One of the first architectural design priorities set by the author, encouraged by many of his fel-

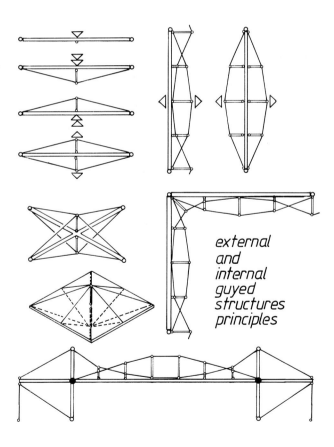

4 Derivation of guyed structures in cross section applicable to space structures with glass panels as the main structural elements and cross bars plus tensile rods as auxiliaries.

low architects, is to develop structures with minimal visual disturbances. As a result, visually minimal two-dimensional structures (so-called because of the flat plates). such as guyed structures, are the most logical of structures. Figure 4 showing the derivation of the guyed structure principle needs no explanation. The principle behind guyed glass structures is that short and slender metal compression bars are used along with long thin metal tension bars and glass plates where invisible normal stresses in the form of tension or compression stresses are included. Fig 4 shows the difference between open and closed structural schemes, of importance in regard to the connections with the substructure. An indication too is given of single-sided and double-sided schemes arising out of architectural considerations, and of the need to stabilize with counterspanning guy trusses when both positive and negative perpendicular loadings have to be accommodated.

Although the structural principle is now established, it seems advisable to develop new aspects and tackle new difficulties at a modest speed; step by step, where every step means only one or two new aspects compared with the in-house technical state of the art. The second part of this book is devoted to this process. The step-by-step method is the only logical way of developing a new technology with modest budgets above the level of the state of the art. Usually only after establishing this technology will the respective standards be developed. The involvement in an earlier phase of positive product research by the official building research institutes would be most welcome. Sometimes, however, when these institutes are invited to participate, their cautious and sometimes conservative advice tends to slow down a new development instead of stimulating it, as their attitude usually is one of extreme cautiousness, with no risks being taken, an attitude that leads to long delays because of the necessary time involved in acquiring new knowledge from research (see par 19).

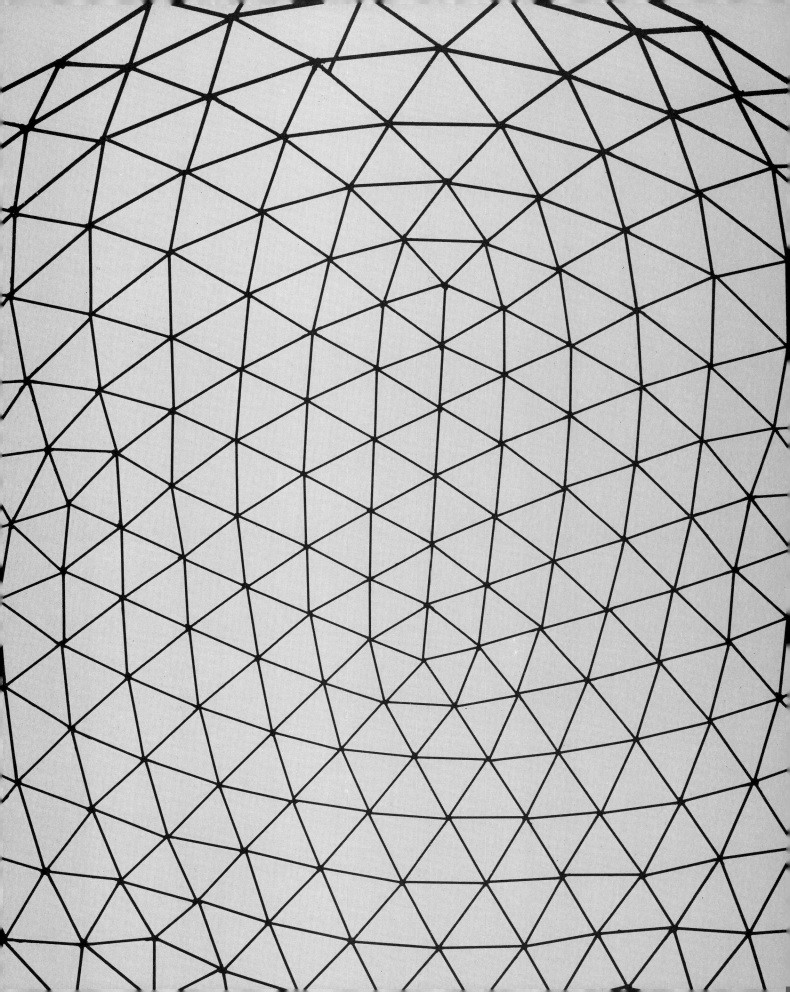

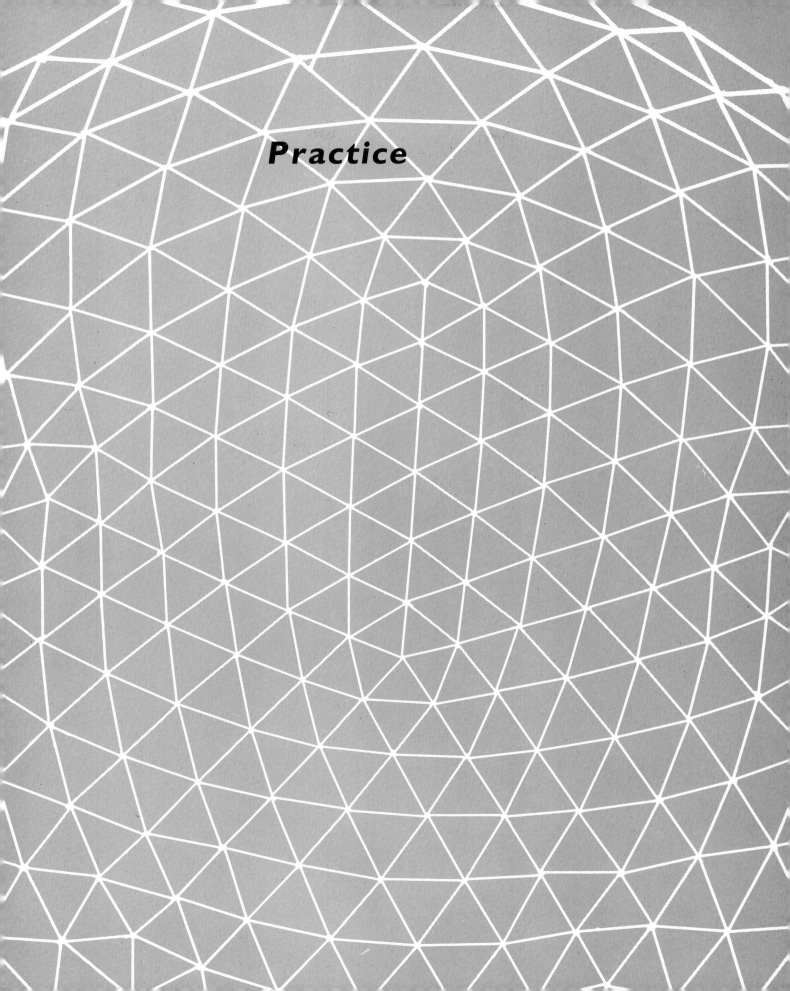

Practice

5, 6, 7 Pictures of the space frame and skylight covering the shopping centre atrium of the Raffles City Complex in Singapore. The basement space is 30 m high and 30 m wide. The lines of the skylight follow the lines of the space frame in projection, keeping enough distance for gutters, drainage slopes ets. The result is a double lining.

9 Space Frames with Separate Glazing Systems

In the building industry, employing a separate metal (steel or aluminium) glazing system around or on a space frame is an accepted solution, ready for sub-contracting. This might be termed 'the traditional approach'. These standard solutions are suitable for normal applications, and in general have the advantage of low costs, but often fail technically when geometric complications arise. In fact in many cases it appeared that standard solutions and more experimental (or non-standard) solutions to certain design problems are worlds apart and show great differences in approach. For example suspended glass surfaces and irregular geometric surfaces and facets usually require non-standard solutions. Apart from that, the resulting optical doubling of structural bars and glazing mullions can be very confusing, and annoying to many architects, especially when the pattern of the space frame differs from that of the skylight.

Raffles City Atrium, Singapore

Within this traditional framework the author developed a new complete glazing system for the Raffles City Glass Atria in Singapore, 1983 (see figs 5 to 7.)

The Raffles City Complex consists of four skyscrapers with two hotels (Westinn Plaza) and offices, more than 75 storeys high and on a basement containing offices, restaurants and a large glass atrium shopping complex. This basement, 30 m high, had to be spanned by steel space frames covered by a flat aluminium glazing system, in panel sizes approximating the space frame modules 1.8 x 1.8 m. There were four different roof elements, 30 x 30 m in size and half that size, cut diagonally. The triangular roof areas had vertical space frame walls to be clad with a similar glass system. To make it even more complicated, the sloped area between the flat and vertical sections had a triangular subdivision (as a projection of the inner space frames) of 1.8 x 1.8 x 1.8 m. The glazing had to be in double glass panels, with an upper panel of 10 mm clear tempered glass, a 12 mm air cavity and a lower panel of laminated clear glass of 5.5.2. Solar protection was in the form of an internal fixed and permanent clear anodized aluminium sunscreen system of small parallel aluminium tubes 30 mm in diameter and placed at 20 mm intervals. Because of the angle of only 4 degrees in the horizontal roof areas and the frequent heavy rainfall in Singapore, the skylight system had to contain an internal drainage system to drain away eventual leakage water. There was no danger of internal condensation as the shopping centre was air-conditioned, so that condensation would only occur on the outside. This specification brief of I.M.Pei & Partners of New York led originally at the tender stage to a skylight system composed of West German Kawneer aluminium sections. However, after one year of in-house development, discussions with Frits Sulzer (I.M.Pei's glazing specialist and a former student of Konrad Wachsmann) and mock-up testing at the TNO Research Institute in Delft, the final Octatube skylight system contained only two standard Kawneer extrusion sections. When development was completed there were seventeen new sections that carried out the required task perfectly. The sections were so designed that leakage water would be able to run from a higher section into a lower one, from a horizontal to a slanting one and finally into a vertical section, down into the outside gutters. Water simply follows the law of gravity in this matter, so the levels were in fact draining off much the same way as a traditional tile roof. The glass panels were 1.65 x 1.8 m, almost the same size as the modules of the space frame below, except for the 0.3 m gutter width and were designed to be screwed onto the main aluminium sections with stainless steel screws through rubbered screw strips. Normally the horizontal screw strips pose the most dangerous leakage problems, as the rainwater has to stream downwards over them. Here they could not be avoided as the design required square glass panels that necessarily had to be screwed on all four sides. In the case of glass panels half that size (for example 0.9 x 1.8 m), the two parallel longer vertical sides could be screwed, while the upper and lower shorter sides could be left unscrewed, and sealed watertight with silicone or silicone band. In these cases it may not be necessary to structurally fix the glass panel on the aluminium supporting section as the span is short and the double glass panel is very rigid. Making these shorter sides watertight is easier, as there are no screws that puncture the waterproof silicone band glued onto the horizontal glass edges. (Which in principle is proof of 'cock-eyed' thinking: puncturing something that has been made watertight with a great deal of effort). These principles are extremely important in the development of all kinds of new glass roofing systems. After completion of the engineering, the design drawings were approved by Fritz Sulzer and sent for production of the dice. From the first trial extrusions a lifesize mock-up was made at the TNO institute at Delft (fig 8). The test was performed with static over- and underpressure and dynamic overpressure. The static pressure was effected by a large compressor, working in a windproof box behind the skylight mock-up. The dynamic overpressure was generated by four aeroplane propellors in a free-standing steel skeleton. Simultaneously water was sprayed on the facade which, depending on the pressure generated, even tended to creep upwards, and, due to an internal underpressure make unexpected assaults on the watertightness of the system.

8 Testing the full size mock-up of the Raffles City space frame and skylight at the TNO Research Institute in Delft.

This procedure was prescribed by I.M.Pei & Partners who exhibited a high level of expertise. Did their desire to be experts on curtain walling and skylighting start with 'the plywood skyscraper'? It almost seems to be the same story as the impulse Ove Arup received from the struggle with the shells of the Sydney Opera House of Jørn Utzon; Ove Arup is now one of the best structural engineering firms in the world with a highly esteemed speciality in spatial structures. From the American tradition of tall buildings it appeared to be easier to work down to a basement skylight system, a more comfortable approach at least than our Dutch way of working upwards, having far less experience with high buildings and their behaviour.

In the case of the Raffles skylight system, there was no alternative than to develop a separate skylight system on a separate space frame, as this space frame was very heavily loaded (high upward and downward wind forces caused by the four large towers), and allowed to rest on only three or four points enabling the towers to move freely without the danger of crushing the space frame. The four large towers gave another problem during the installation of the space frame and skylight. Objects thrown casually from above proved to be very dangerous: falling bolts but also food re-

mains had the effect of ammunition. Falling scaffolding pipes became spears. The Korean project contractor Ssang Yong clearly had to cope with a lack of discipline in his large crew. After finishing the skylights a nice 'Moiré effect' can be observed between the sunscreen and the space frame tubes during the day, in counterlight. At night because of the internal lighting the atrium volumes seem to be closed off and show a shiny aluminium skin. To obtain another effect at will, the architect has built on the outside of the horizontal roof (in the gutter) light fittings, giving the same gloom at night as during the day, and a romantic overview seen from the upper hotel room balconies. The photograph 9 shows the graphic play of lines of the space frame lining and the skylight lining.

10 *Space Frames with Integrated Glazing*

Designing with lightweight structures often means the chance of an elegant and fragile structure built up of small diameter tubes. Often the aluminium skylight mullions in rectangular hollow sections seem thicker than the slender round steel tubes of the space frame. The interference of two different graphic systems, either with elements in two independent geometric systems (as is usually the case, see fig 10), or even parallel (Raffles City skylight, see fig 9), can be so disturbing that it stimulates efforts to get the two graphic systems in one line. So the first step from the traditional skylight as an independent system on the space frame towards structural glass, was to design and develop an integrated system in which the glazing mullions coincide with the space frame bars. A distinction has to be made here between space frames with square or rectangular modules and space frames with trapezoidal or triangular modules. A definite disadvantage is that the price of trapezoidal but more so of triangular glass panels is more than double that of square or rectangular panels. Thus changing from rectangular to triangular glass panels costs money. But by integrating the skylight mullion and the space frame tube the visual aspect has been improved 100%. Continuing this train of thought, the Tuball space frame system has spawned a new line of sections known as OT-sections, in which the functions of structure and cladding are clearly legible: the circular part carries normal forces, the T-flange on top carries the glass (or cladding) panel. The system as a whole is called the Tuball-Plus system (fig 11), and is made of aluminium. The special machining-out of the ends of the aluminium elements enable us to place the cap on top of the spherical shell after tightening the bolts (during the tightening itself there is as much room for

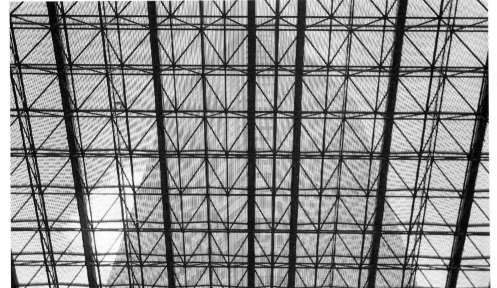

9 Interior picture of the atrium skylights of the Raffles City Complex in Singapore.

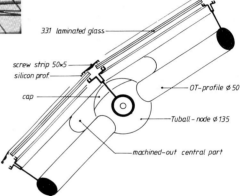

331 laminated glass

screw strip 50×5

silicon prof.

cap

OT-profile ø 50

Tuball-node ø 135

machined-out central part

11 Drawing of a Tuball-Plus joint with a spherical node and OT profiles to accommodate the cladding panels (glass/metal).

10 Typical example of a space frame with separate skylight (Almatrium, Nieuwegein NL: 43.2 × 43.2 m).

the screwdrivers and wrenches as a dentist sometimes has when drilling a back tooth) but it is also designed as a clear expression of the form of the sphere, separate from the OT-sections. The circular silhouette-form follows the fluid circular lines of the sphere.

The Haarlem Music Dome

The music dome in Haarlem, designed by the then town architect Wiek Röling in collaboration with the author as a structural designer, was built in 1984 as the first application of a Tuball-Plus system of integrated structure and cladding elements (fig 12). This dome is a geodesic dome with a three-frequency icosahedronal subdivision. All glass panels have the same triangular form as the structure. Fig 13 gives an inside view. The design of the Tuball-Plus node with ma-

12 Overall view of the music pavilion geodesic dome in Haarlem, 9 m wide, 7.5 m high. A three-frequency icosahedron. Rib length ± 1.7 m, covered with laminated clear glass in the Tuball-Plus system.

13 Inside view of the glass-clad Haarlem Music Dome.

chined-out bar ends began life as a flash of inspiration at the drawing board, strongly influenced by the possibilities of a prototype laboratory. For the sake of completeness one should mention two typical technical contradictions, giving some idea of the immanent battle between the system's designer and structural engineer. Firstly it is not customary to introduce bending stresses in the space frame bars other than the normal stresses. Secondly at the place where the largest shear forces are acting because of the bending moments, most of the material at the end of the OT-bars has been machined away. These interventions derive from the stress analysis of the different elements, but visually to the structural engineer they seem illogical. Here it was the product-architect who made the decision, and created a 'design' detail instead of a structural one. The design of the Haarlem Music Dome was so highly appreciated that it received the first Dutch Aluminium Award in 1986.

Octagonal Domes, Germany

Later more designs followed, including standard shallow domes on an octagonal base, specially developed for West Germany. The West German architectural market is one where consequence and systemizing predominate. So consistent designs are much appreciated: with angles of 90/45 degrees German domes seem preferably to be octagonal in plan. The size of the first two domes was approximately 6 m; the insulated glass panels were triangular (see fig 14). They were designed in 1988 by the author and built for several car showrooms.

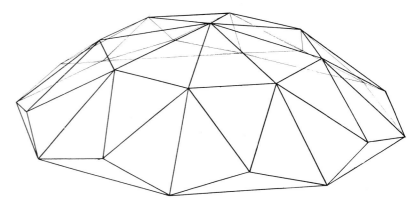

14 Isometric view of an Octagonal Tuball-Plus dome used for car showrooms in Germany.

Tanfield House Domes, Edinburgh

A different design has been made for three similar shallow 15 m domes in a network geometry of horizontal rings of OT-sections with triangulated OT-bracings in-between. The angles between the individual elements at the nodes perpendicular to the imaginary enveloping sphere are strong enough to allow for a single-layered dome. The three domes have been built to vault circular atria in the open office landscaping of the head office of the Standard Life Insurance Company in Edinburgh. The lower 24 nodes are supported on 12 columns (leaving 12 more flexible supported nodes). The project architect is John Perreur Lloyd of Michael Laird & Partners (fig 15,16). The domes in Tuball-Plus have been covered with light silver reflective insulated glass panels and made watertight by a silicone band sealed with silicone and secured by aluminium screw strips on top. Moreover each dome has an external and an internal ladder for maintenance and glass cleaning, and a rotating automated sunscreen system, covering the southernmost 240 degrees according to the time of the day and the measured intensity of solar energy (winter/summer).

Serangoon Gardens Country Club, Singapore

One of the most complex designs realized after the development of the Tuball-Plus system, not in triangulated but in rectangulated form, was the atrium covering for the Serangoon Gardens Country Club in Singapore. The project architect, Eugene Seow of Akitek Tenggara in Singapore had designed a building consisting of two symmetrical terraced reinforced concrete structures in three storeys with an intermediate atrium 21 x 35 m. The covering of the atrium was originally conceived as cylindrical in acrylic material, but the architect insisted upon a column-free space, and was not particularly taken by the acrylic morphology and properties. The author's alternative proposal was to make four intermediate linear gutters built between double I-beams and to build a system of triangular space trusses on top of these gutter edges in the Tuball-Plus system (much the same as later realized in the Amsterdam arcade, see figs 20,21). The space frame module size was a full glass panel size (1.7 x 1.7 m). The design of this system of five adjacent cylindrical barrel vaults was adapted to the respective heights of the adjacent concrete terraced roof levels, see figs 17 to 19. After receipt of the contract, however, the project engineer discovered that there was no possibility of connecting the ends of the structural gutters to the concrete frame, as there were lightly reinforced balconies cantilevering from the same structure at the same place – a professional error. So at that

15 Outside view of one of the three similar 15 m diameter shallow atrium domes for the Standard Life head office in Edinburgh.

16 Inside view with the inside and outside ladder and fully automated rotating solar screens, all fixed on a central axis, stabilized by guy rods and running on outside circular tube rails.

moment the decision was made to change the structural system into five independent complete space frames acting as shells, supported only at the four corner nodes, with suspended non-structural gutters in-between. The responsibility in this contract included not only the space structure, but also the glass panels, ventilation louvres, gutters, electronically operating internal sunscreen systems and electric exhaust fans. Octatube was nominated sub-contractor with co-design duties, but with little additional influence on the rest of the building. The overall design of the building has strong Structuralist influences in the composition of the independent concrete floor areas each supported by four corner columns, ending with four columns at each column position, even at the outer corners of the building. The space frame anticipated that scheme. On the other hand, the

17, 18, 19 Pictures of the glass atrium of the Serangoon Gardens Country Club in Singapore as 5 shell-like barrel vaulted space frames with glazing on OT-profiles in module size 1.7 × 1.7 m.

architect's interest in the structural behaviour and the details of the space frame design, especially in its spatial character and the complex 3-D details, stimulated the product-architect to optimize the frame details and elements. The end result is a glass waterfall on the outside and a complex spatial structure which cannot be viewed at one glance, on the inside. The ventilation in this glass atrium is natural, cooled off by the chimney-effect of instreaming air from the swimming pool side. We found, however, that the ventilation louvres in the gutters did not function well because incoming air was warmed up outside by the radiating grey-tinted single glass panels in the gutter area. In fact we were ventilating with heated air. A better idea would have been to open the gables of the five barrel vaults completely and close off the ventilation louvres. The glass panels were laminated 6.6.2 panels with the outer pane grey-tinted and tempered, and the inner pane float glass. Practically all panels damaged during transport and installation were broken in the float glass panel, and not in the tempered panel. Because of the anticipated temperature elongations in the glass panels and also in the space structure, the space frame supports on one side of the building were made sliding, so that no extra thermal forces would be introduced in the space frame, or in the glass panels. This complex Gothic cathedral-like five-bayed glass atrium was awarded a second Dutch Steel Prize in 1986, although half its elements were made of aluminium OT-sections (i.e. the upper chord members).

20 Outside view of the central arcade on the shopping centre 'De Amsterdamse Poort' in Amsterdam-Zuidoost, with an adjacent shallow dome covered with sandwich and glass panels.

21 Inside view of the Amsterdamse Poort arcade, displaying the composition of triangular trusses with module 1.7 × 1.7 m, covered by laminated glass panels the same size. Delta trusses every 3.4 m. The arcade forms with its width of 11 m and height of 5.5 m an homage to the semi-cylindrical 19th century shopping centre glass roofs, but made more abstract with minimal material.

Amsterdamse Poort Arcade, Amsterdam

In the shopping centre 'De Amsterdamse Poort' in Amsterdam, a glazed arcade has been designed by architect Ben Loerakker and the author, comprising triangular Tuball-Plus trusses spanning 11 m, with a total length in the arcade of 34 m and a height of 5.5 m. The single glass panels in this amply ventilated arcade are laminated 3.3.1 and the module size 1.7 m (see figs 21,22). Although this design has the definite advantage of clear glass panels as large as the space frame modules, and fits correctly into the development process of this book, later designs (like a similar cylindrical arcade in Mönchengladbach, Germany, 70 x 5.1 m and up to 10 m high) made use of a more failsafe system of additional vertical aluminium sections, so that the insulated glass panels could be screwed at the side and glued or taped off horizontally. Visually this resulted in less refinement than was anticipated. The Amsterdam glass arcade has a similar form to the 19th century shopping arcades (compare fig 1), but is a very lightweight, minimal, yet abstract and spatial variation on this century-old theme. This scheme was enabled by the availability of two continuous supports on both sides of the arcade, so that in fact arched structures were made, far different in action from that of the Serangoon space frame shell. Visually it is much simpler, less complex than the complete space frames built in the Serangoon Gardens Country Club atrium structure.

11 Space Frames with Structurally Sealed Glass

A further step forward is to replace the mechanical screw connection between glass and structure with a structural sealant with silicone, while the watertightness seam is now a separate silicone seal instead of a rubber strip (fig 22). So in this case there are two types of sealant: structural adhesive, and weather seal separated by a foamband so that structural movements in two directions can function independently. The result is a flush outside surface without any screw strips, giving the dome an even more crystalline character, while all irregularities encouraging the adherence of dirt to the surface have been removed. Colour of the structural seal is important here: black, being the most uv-resistant, is too strong a colour when glass is clear. Grey-tinted glass and a grey seal form a better harmony.

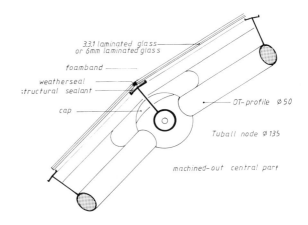

22 Detail of a Tuball-Plus node suitable for silicone sealed glass panels.

Prinsenhof Dome, Delft

A further example is the design in 1987 by the author of a music dome pavilion for the Prinsenhof in Delft (fig 23). This structure is a 6 m dome designed as a 4-frequency (exploded) octahedron. This polyhedron has the advantage of a composition of eight identical parts. Thus a complete sphere can be made, or 7/8, 6/8, even as little as 1/8. In the case of the Prinsenhof dome a hemisphere was cut into two halves, separated and joined by a strip of glass panels in blue-tinted glass; all other (triangular) glass panels were to be grey-tinted. This blue band was the expression of the borderline between garden and street, which happened to be the location.

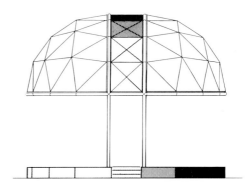

23 Design of a 6/7 m geodesic dome in the geometry of two quarters of an exploded octahedral sphere in clear glass, connected with a central support zone in grey-tinted glass, as a music bandstand in the Prinsenhof museum, Delft.

Raffles City Entrance, Singapore

Another example is the canopy of the Raffles City Hotel Complex in Singapore, where flat laminated clear glass panels of 6.6.2 were sealed directly onto the aluminium Tuball-Plus sections. The flat roof plane has a camber of only 1%. On top of the space frame square panels were used; on the sides, triangular panels. The outside of the triangular glass panels forms one flush glass surface 1.5 x 42 m long. The module length is 1.9 m (fig 24,25).

By the virtue of the hollow sphere and circular sections extra holes drilled in the nodes and tube ends enable electric cables to be fed through so that fittings with concealed wires can be combined. In other projects tungsten-halogen lamps have been built in that are hardly visible when switched off (ca 10 mm in size!), while the transformers were built in the spherical nodes.

Maritime Museum, Maasbracht

An identical effect in the glass surface was obtained for the space frame glazing at the Maritime Museum in Maasbracht, designed by architect Maarten Engelman and the author (figs 26,27). The size of the space frame above the architect's office on the 3rd floor of this museum is 18 x 18 m; the module is 1.5 m. The single glass panels 6 mm thick are screwed on upper and lower sides; the vertical 6 mm joints are merely sealed with silicone. This configuration was chosen in particular from a large number of alternatives as it shows the internal space frame in all its graphic beauty and bright green colour without any glazing mullion lines disturbing the surface of the glass in a horizontal direction.

24, 25 Pictures of the entrance canopy for the Raffles City complex in Singapore, where a Tuball-Plus space frame was designed with structurally sealed flat (1% slope) laminated glass panels 1.8 × 1.8 m. The water drips on the glass surface indicate a flat roof position. Designed by architect I.M.Pei, detailled by the author.

26 Interior view of a corner of the Maritime Museum glazing: single toughened glass silicone sealed horizontally, with upper and lower continuous screw strips, to give the image of one 18 m long horizontal glassplate.

27 Exterior view of the Maritime Museum and
architects (top floor) office, designed by architect
Maarten Engelman.

28 Overall picture of entrance lobby of the Zalmhaven office in Rotterdam by architect Han Steke-
tee and the author (1989) with double glass panels
and central Quattro studs supporting the glass panels in the middle.

29, 30 The entrance canopy of the Almatrium in
Nieuwegein NL as a free-standing space frame
slightly sloped, covered by laminated glass panels
max 1.6 m wide; the glass panels are supported
centrally by saucer struts. Design by architect Jan
van Rooijen (ZZOP) and the author.

Central Supports for Glass Panels on Space Frames

Two more projects have been realized with siliconed flat glass panels on top of a Tuball space frame: the entrance to the Zalmhaven office building in Rotterdam and the entrance to the Almatrium complex in Nieuwegein, Netherlands. These two projects were used to experiment with relatively thin, large glass sheets, supported around the four edges and also centrally to reduce bending moments in the glass plate, preventing staining of the glass through dried rainwater and dust areas in the deflecting centres of the panels. In both cases the glass panels were determined by the optimal size of the modules in the space frame (1.5/1.6 m), and were actually too large for regular glass thicknesses of 3.3.1. In order to keep a reasonably low dead weight on the glass, an intermediate vertical stud was developed to support the centres of the individual glass panels, and detailed in principle with a Quattro or 'frog-finger'-like support head similar to that used for the Glass Music Hall in Amsterdam (see par 16) to minimize support tensions. In the Octa Lab tests were carried out to determine the impact resistance of the double glass panels supported by a central Quattro node by bags of metal grit of different weight falling from different heights. The metal-on-glass connection is glued here to resist the small horizontal sliding forces. In a later phase a double-sided tape might be used. The Zalmhaven roof has insulated glass panels (figs 28,29); the Almatrium canopy only single laminated glass panels (fig 30). The Zalmhaven roof has double glazing; the Quattro support points of the lower glass panels are continued by means of nylon 12 mm props in the air cavity between the two panels to support the upper panel. One aspect of the Almatrium canopy has led to considerable study: as this canopy is not heated in winter, there is the danger of an ice layer forming on the glass. As long as the ice can expand freely there is no problem. But this design has two sloping halves that drain off into an intermediate gutter. Ice building up in the gutter could be disastrous because of the danger of expansion. Therefore a deep gutter detail was developed with the advice to combine electric cables in it to prevent ice at all times.

The author has recently proposed another scheme for an entrance canopy, where a flat double layered space frame will be used with module / glass panel size 2.7 x 2.7 m, being the largest commercially available square laminated glass panels possible in 4.4.2 (see fig 31). This size of glas panels minimizes the amount of weather seals necessary. In order to reduce deflections due to deadweight and external loadings, the glass panels are supported by four additional field sup-

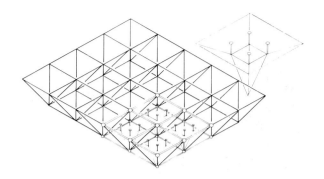

31 Design proposal detail of a flat Tuball space frame entrance canopy (total size 13.5 × 10,8 m) in space frame modules 2.7 × 2.7 m. The horizontal glass panels 4.4.2. measure 2.7 × 2.7 m and are supported by 4 counteracting suspended poles glued under the glass panels. This glass size allows the maximal sizes of regular space frame elements and of laminated glass panels.

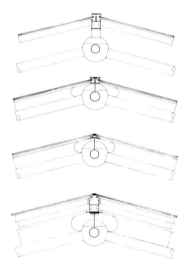

32 Tuball-Plus joint with mechanically screwed glass panels with prefabricated silicone sealed aluminium profiles, made watertight by a locally applied silicone seal. Advantage: weather-independent application. Glass must be tinted to hide the mechanical connections.

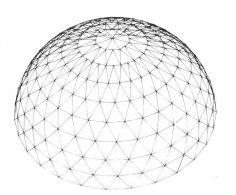
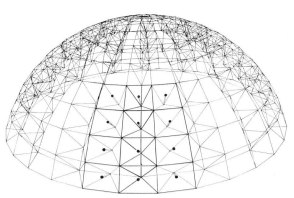

33, 34 Two alternative overall views of a 30 m dome for the world Trade Centre in Bangkok, with underspanned laminated single glass panels, with max side lengths of 3.0 m.

ports: small steel saucers under laminated circular glass plates for stress concentration, glued on the glass surface, hinging on top of short steel compression poles dia 25 mm that are underspanned by four tensile rods dia 10 mm leading to the four adjacent upper chord nodes to resist downward loadings. In order to cope with the upward loading either a similar arrangement can be made aboven the glass (which has the problem of perforating the watertight glass surface in the seams), resp the four poles are spanned downward towards the central lower chord node of the space frame. Similar arrangements for stiffening other designs of glass panels can be used provided counterspanning tensile rod crossings are used both for upward as for downward loadings Its principle of counterspanning cables is similar to the description of stretched membranes [see par 5.2 of ref 1].

Glueing glass panels with a structural sealant on the building site is not a real gain for assembly technology but a building method highly sensitive to low temperatures and varying humidity/wetness. Further development, therefore, led to glass elements provided in the factory (under ideal climatic conditions) with glued-on aluminium sections with a structural sealant, to be screwed mechanically to the structure on site, and subsequently weathersealed with silicone when the humidity allows it (fig 33,34). Unfortunately in this case the visual section thickness is greater and the detailing no longer has an acceptable slenderness as in the Tu-ball-Plus designs.

Following the development of the additional central Quattro-stud for support of thin glass plates, a design has been made for an all-glass dome of 30 m diameter, 10 m height on top of the World Trade Centre in Bangkok (fig 34). The triangulated subdivision of OT-sections is necessarily a large-scale one to prevent the dome from the dangers of local buckling (long rib lengths and steeper corners mean less danger of local buckling). The flat glass panels are very thick where rib lengths of 3.2 m are developed. Here, too, the

proposal was to use an intermediate central Quattro support stud suspended by three cables to the three adjacent space frame nodes.

12 Space Frames and Stabilizing Sealed Glass

The next step after the structural sealing of glass panels now seems logical. The idea is to give the glass panels an extra horizontal stabilizing function in the form of additional shear strength. At present it should be possible to design a rectangulated single-layered hinged space frame, where the horizontal stability can be borne by the glass panels sealed with structural sealant on the metal frame, preventing horizontal deformations. The consequence of this is that not only triangulated domes and saddle-shaped structures can be built but also rectangulated or trapezoidal subdivisions, which are cheaper than the triangulated structures because of the cheaper cladding. (Triangulated glass panels are 2.0 to 2.6 times as expensive as rectangular or square panels, and so are more decisive to costs than the structure itself. In general, too, one could state that the covering skylights are more expensive that the space frame underneath.)

19th Century Glass Houses

Using the shear strength of glass panels is an idea that was used unconsciously in the last century in glass houses. These glass panels ensured most of the horizontal stability because they were fixed in rigid putty. Detailed study of these glass houses, such as the Crystal Art Palace in the Botanical Gardens in Glasgow, show in the curvatures of the domes with their horizontally twisted lines (fig 35) that the shear resistance came from the glass panels and not from the metal structure below. There are no metal wind bracings in these structures.

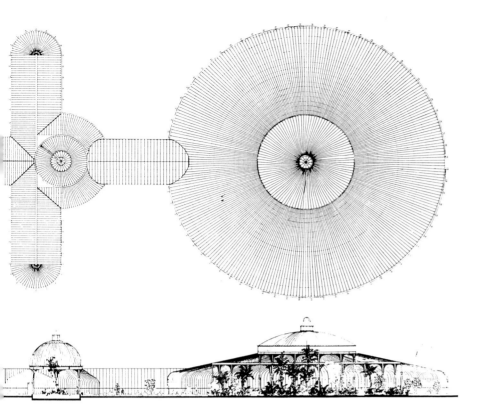

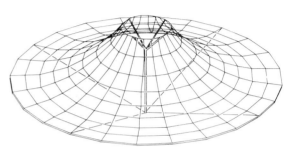

Glass Tents

One example is a proposal for a tent-like polygonal atrium skylight pretensioned by a central hanging mast and guying cables designed by the author in 1989 (fig 36). Delft civil engineering student Henny ter Huerne designed in 1990 as part of his final studies, assisted by the author, a composition of four identical glass tent structures based on an octagonal plan form with square space frames in the intermediate areas (see fig 37). The macrostructural system consists of suspended masts and guy elements in two directions to give enough rigidity for downward, upward and asymmetrical loading. The glass panels are silicone sealed on the metal tent frame and take care of local horizontal stability. The vertical local stability of the tent is effected by vertical pretensioning and by horizontal continuous purlin members.

Transworld Marine Dome, Rotterdam

The first real application of the principle of lateral stability given by glass panels to a metal space frame structure will be the dome on top of the Rotterdam branch office of Transworld Marine designed by architect Pieter de Boer of Haskoning Architects and Engineers. This sphere houses a recreational facility on the sixth floor of the office building, but is also a symbol of the company's logo: a sphere made of circles

36 A tent-like glass skylight pre-tensioned by a central hanging mast. The glass panels take care of the horizontal stability (torsion), as designed by the author in 1989. Glass could have different colours.

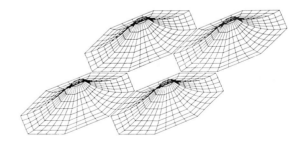

37 Design model by Delft civil engineering student Henny ter Huerne of four identical glass tent elements in octagonal plan, covering an atrium of 42 × 42 m. Glass covering by double glass panels.

of latitude and altitude, in reality meridional and radial metal space frame elements, clad with quadrangular glass panels. The central problem to overcome here was to prove that the glass bonding on the space frame elements also retains its strength in the long term (see fig 38). As we did not find a sealant manufacturer who could assure us of this, the structural analysis involved three levels of action. Firstly the rigidity of the aluminium Tuball-Plus dome, enabling small bending moments on each node perpendicular to the glass plane; secondly, the glass panels bonded on the OT-sections, giving stability to the dome in the plane of the glass panels; thirdly the wedging-in of the quadrangular double glass panels between the OT-sections with nylon glass blocks, so that shear forces could be taken over mechanically. It was felt that these three modes of action will not take place simultaneously. Rather, before a too large deformation in the metal frame takes place (1), the glass plates will stiffen the structure (2) and eventual long-run deformation is prevented by the glass wedges (3). The fact that the dome is a 3/4 sphere and cantilevers over the building means an extra structural challenge with a higher degree of difficulty as to accessibility for the maintenance crew.

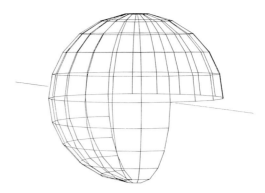

38 Isometry of the Transworld Marine 3/4 sphere of 7 m diameter on top of an office building in Rotterdam.

13 *Spoked Glass Panels*

During the development of many skylight systems and applications, the author tried to combine structural design and skylight detailing. One of the results was an application of aluminium skylights with greater lengths than that of one glass panel, and replacement of the obligatory supporting purlin by an underspanning stud and two or more underspanning cables or rods. This supporting system is a very old theme: in the last century timber/iron trusses were formed like this, and were known as 'Polonceau trusses' after their inventor. It is merely a question of rediscovery and application in three-dimensional terms with an interesting spatial effect, rather than the simple, heavy and not particularly elegant truss-and-purlin method of traditional steel designers. Fig 39 shows such an example of underspanned timber skylights, for the Limburg provincial government building in Hasselt, Belgium, designed by the late Professor Ludwig van Wilder and the author. Underspanned skylights are but a small step forward in the pursuit of elegant structural design. But the underspanning principle, once applied, has led to another way of thinking. It provided extra means of stabilizing weak elements with studs and rods. It is only a very simple step forward from glass panels stabilizing space frames to the stabilization of glass panels by metal components. But in doing so the importance of the two elements

39 Underspanned Skylight in Hasselt (B) with timber rafters, steel underspanning elements and aluminium skylights on top.

almost seems to be reversed: glass plates now have the primary and metal components the secondary and part-primary function. So this step is the most crucial one in the process described in this book as it turned the normal way of thinking upside-down!

Osaka Pavilions

The most simple form is an assembly of four glass panels in a metal frame which are fixed in the centre by two cross bars, stabilized in their turn by 2 x 4 tensile bars to the four corners. The whole resembles a square bicycle wheel with 2 x 4 spokes (fig 40). The central nave really consists of two half-elements compressing together the glass panels in-between.

The seams between two adjacent panels are formed by acrylate H-sections that even give no shadow line and are almost invisible. This system has been designed as the glass facade of a modular exhibition hall for the Dutch pavilion built in Osaka in March 1989 for the EVD (a PR service of the Dutch Ministry of Economic Affairs) by project architect Frans Prins and the author (fig 42). A similar pavilion was later built there in a slightly modified form for Heineken Japan in March 1990, also in Osaka. The original design consists of a modular Tuball space frame in portal form 4.8 m high, 9.6 m deep and 19.2 m long. All three space frame planes are covered with white prestressed PVC/PS membrane elements, while the long fascias are covered with the above stabilized glass system. If the system were to be built without the surrounding metal frame, the glass panels would be compressed in their plane towards each other, with the acrylate H-sections in-between. The Osaka pavilions have been purposely designed as an ode to traditional Japanese modular architecture in a modern form, with modern materials and modern techniques, and a touch of Western High-Tech. Space frame buildings and traditional Japanese architecture have a strong modular character in common: modularity as a restriction, but with a particular design freedom in every application, so no two buildings ever have to look alike. The requirement of quick site assembly and demountability has led to the specific choices of materials and components. The module had to be 2.4 m everywhere, as the Japanese appeared to be very strict in the use of regulations. As the shipping container size is outwardly 2.4 m but inwardly 2.2 m, glass panels sized 2.4 x 2.4 m could not be transported but had to be divided into four. So the size of the glass panels is 1.2 x 1.2 m in demountable window frames of 2.4 x 2.4 m. As a consequence of the design of the Tuball space frame, the nodal point of the top of the cross bars has the hollow sphere-form into which the four spokes run and can be prestressed internally without visible nuts. This underlines the abstract character of the design.

The second, 'Heineken' version was slightly smaller, 14.4 x 9.6 m, and had a built-in veranda and a glass wall in two perpendicular planes of 4.8 x 4.8 m. To save exhibition space the lower nodes and tubes of the walls were replaced by columns. This second version was provided with in-built double derricks, as additional assembly means were impossible to get in Osaka because of the high degree of bureaucracy in Japan in general and the always desperately busy exhibition building sites; and as the time available for complete installation was only five days.

Following on from this development another arrangement was designed composed of nine glass panels each 1.8 x 1.8 m, thus totalling 5.4 x 5.4 m, stabilized by 2 x 4 cross bars and 2 x 4 guy cables (fig 41). The compression forces were taken by the glass panels and a surrounding RHS section, while the guy cables acted under tension. The connections had the same simplicity. This composition was conceived for the occasion of a Booosting TV display in April 1989. To show the structural strength a Dutch break-dance act was staged on the glass floor in the TV studio.

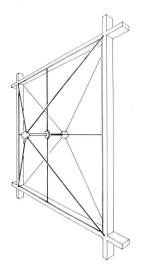

40 Prototype of a single window frame composed of 4 different square glass panels in a steel frame, where the central joint has been stabilized by two central studs and 2 × 4 tensile rods. The joints between the glass panels are made of transparent acrylic H-Profiles.

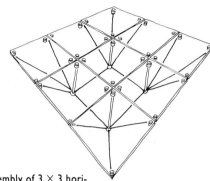

41 Design proposal of an assembly of 3 × 3 horizontal glass panels stabilized by underspanned guy rods as a break-dancing floor for the Brandpunt TV programme.

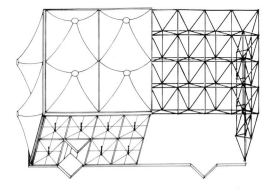

42 The Osaka EVD pavilion consisting of a tunnel-shaped space frame, clad with stretched membrane elements as a tribute to traditional Japanese architecture; the front fascia elements are composed of units built up of four stabilized glass panels, with two cross bars and 2 × 4 spokes. Designed by architect Frans Prins and the author (1988).

14   *Prestressed Glass Panels*

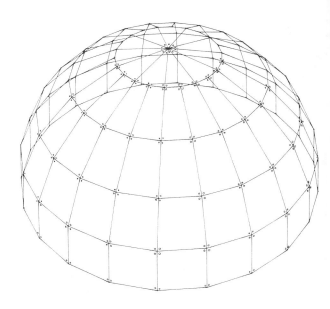

Of considerable influence on the subject of this book were the Dutch project architects Peter Gerssen and Cas Oosterhuis who wanted to design an all-glass dome structure with a 30 m span at Schiphol Airport, Amsterdam. The first response of the author was that this was impossible, but after one week of gnashing the teeth, the attitude became one of living up to the challenge offered by this issue. So their innovative idea was unconsciously the eye-opener for the author as a product-architect in 1987. The actual project (designed by the author, fig 43) was never realized, but the stimulus of the idea was fruitful enough, as the author became determined to reach this goal after an adequate process of design, research and development, and in fact today it would be fully realizable.

The next step in the development process is to give glass panels a true primary structural function, by letting them function to pass normal forces. To that end a thorough theoretical study was made in 1988 at Octatube by Rik Grashoff, a student of Civil Engineering at the TU Delft. The initiative was a result of the dissertation 'Architecture in Space Structures' by the author, begun in January 1988 and published in May 1989 [Ref 1]. The aim of this structural feasibility study was purposely kept to technical aspects, not to financial aspects or acoustic and thermal behaviour, as these aspects were supposed only to restrict and endanger a potential technical step forward. The aim was to build an all-glass structure without steel elements for the external perimeter – thus completely independent.

Flat structures will have to be made double-layered when there is only one loading situation, and triple-layered when there are reverse loading situations such as wind pressure and suction on vertical walls. Roof structures suffer less from vertical uplift, but here asymmetrical loading might be decisive. The glass panels will then always be under compression, while the auxiliary (short) cross bars will be under compression and the cables/rods under tension. Roof structures in cylindrical form may be single-layered, but will have to be reinforced in the zero-curvature direction, as they suffer from local buckling problems in that direction. As this type of construction is very popular, its systemized structural glass application is under study at this moment (June 1990). Dome-formed structures can be made entirely single-layered without additional cross bars and guy cables when the spans are modest and the curvatures steep (the corners between two adjacent glass panels more than 3 – 5°).

The material investigation showed indeed that glass is still the only appropriate structural transparent material for

43 Design proposal for a 30 m diameter glass dome for the Schiphol Airport Hotel, designed by the author for Cas Oosterhuis and Peter Gerssen.

systems of the type described above (see par 6). For safety reasons tempered glass panels in roofs could be laminated and used as structural plates, although the lamination layer weakens the structural capacity by 30 %. Single tempered glass is unsafe (depending on the risk of vandalism and estimations of mechanical loadings and fall height). Duplex-strengthened glass has problems with accuracies in the position of bolt holes and panel sizes. Laminated normal glass is as safe, but less expensive and cannot have bolt holes. The investigation took as its basis thick tempered glass panels laminated with thin normal glass panels for minimum security reasons. Lamination of two tempered glass plates will have to be done by fluid epoxy to fill the more irregular space between these two plates, which can be bent slightly or warped because of their heat treatment. The study resulted in a system of laminated tempered panels in square sizes from 1.0 to 2.1 m, with thicknesses of 6, 8, 10, 12, 15 and 19 mm.

The first prototype connection in 1988 in the material-structural feasibility study was made with four plywood (rather than glass) panels and four double-sided turn buckles to prestress the connection so that both compression and tension forces could be transferred. In order to avoid the danger of asymmetrical prestressing (with bending moments on the glass panels), at the end of the three months' study equilibrium saddles were built into the prototype in order to obtain normal forces in the glass plates even under strong asymmetrical pre-tensioning (fig 44). The total size of this second prototype was 1.9 x 1.9 m, composed of 3 x 3

44 Detail picture of the second mock-up composed of 9 glass panels prestressed by pretension bolts, compression studs and tensile cables. The mock-up was used to examine a new mode of mechanical action in glass structures.

glass panels of 630 x 630 mm (thus in scale 1:3) to be able to carry the prototype as a whole and to use it for exhibition purposes, while the mechanical connection nodes and auxiliaries were made at actual size. The whole assembly gave, as a result of the mixture of scales, a rather mechanical impression, requiring further refinement in design. Another disadvantage of the 1:3 scale of the glass plates was their relative stiffness, transmitting loadings that normally could not have been taken because of the high torsion rigidity of the scale model. The internal prestress method had the aim of overcoming the traditional cutting tolerances of the glass, and to make watertight seams by means of a compressed prefabricated sealant band. In practice these glass tolerances now seem quite satisfactory (see par 16: Glass Music Hall) so that tolerances in the metal components appeared to be most critical. The prestress principle was put forward for patent, but shelved for the time being as there proved to be simpler ways leading to a similarly watertight result. The prestress method proved to be adequate for single layered domes, but in the case of stabilized flat planes one might say that nodal prestressing and prestressing from stabilization cables are doing the same job, so that nodal prestress is in fact redundant.

15 Structural Glass Walls

The first scheme for a prestressed structural curtain wall was designed in 1988 by architect Paul Verhey for a fashion shop of the Cool Cat concern in Groningen, the Netherlands.

Cool Cat Shop, Groningen

The design consists of six panels of 2 x 2.25 m in a total size of 4.5 m high and 6 m width as a suspended glass curtain on the first storey of the shop front, as shown in the perspective drawing in fig 45. The overview and detail of the joint is given in photographs 46 to 47. For this initial application it was assembled in its entirety in the Octatube factory. The evaluation of this mock-up in the laboratory in which both the glass panels and the joints were actual size, proved the visual correctness of the Minimal Material hypothesis. The six panels are assembled into one consistent whole by a double-sided guyed bar system of 2 x 3 cross bars. The size of the short cross bars is 20 mm, the tensile guy bars 8 mm. The size of the glass panels was so large compared with the joints that the latter were enlarged in the design phase out of visual considerations (in order to obtain a visually credible structure) from 40 mm to 50 mm props. The assembly forms a structural entity, in the sense that this closed system contains the necessary tensile and compressive elements to

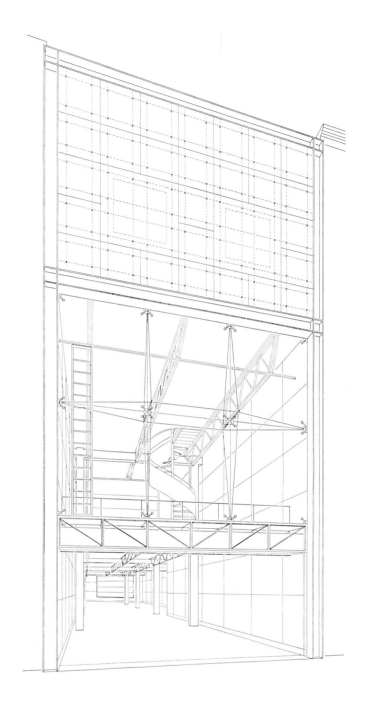

45 Perspective view of the Cool Cat shop in Groningen NL designed in 1988 by architect Paul Verhey. The curtain wall of the first floor (4.5 × 6 m wide) is suspended from the steel portal and transfers the wind forces to the four sides of the glass wall.

46, 47 Details for this suspended certain wall were designed by the author as a simplified solution for fig 44. The nodes are not prestressed, but the overall guy rods prestress the glass plates on compression. Wind loads heighten the compression forces in the glass and the tensile forces in one of the two rod systems, depending on the wind's direction.

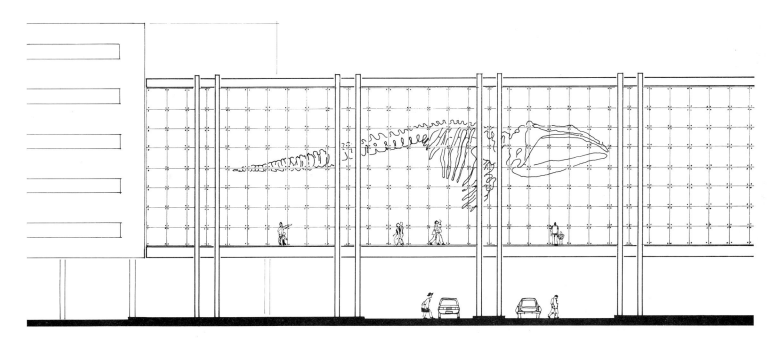

48 Design proposal for a high pedestrian bridge with show case between two biology museum buildings in Leiden NL.

form an independent whole, independent of a surrounding steel substructure. It could also work in space, without additional boundary supports. However, to function in the actual design the structure has been suspended from a steel portal frame. Wind forces are taken to the four sides of the structure; on the lower side a metal bridge takes over the horizontal wind forces in suction and compression, but vertical forces are not taken over due to the vertical sleeve holes. In this way too the extra loads on the bridge cannot cause extra vertical stresses in the curtain wall. The detailing of the nodes, the cross bars and the guy bars is very functional, but abstract in its design. The glass plates are under compression by the prestress mechanism from the stabilizing nodes, while the wind loads result in extra compression forces in the glass plates as well as extra tension in one of the tensile elements. These are the two different mechanisms in operation.

The mock-up in the Octatube factory clearly showed the inspiration derived from such a structure. As regards material application there is no more material than is absolutely necessary. The transparency of the structure underlines one of the evaluation criteria of its product development, i.e. minimum visual disturbance. It also underlines the extra value aimed at in this process: giving structures a certain inspiring form. The late professor Ludwig van Wilder of Delft University gave another point of view when he commented on the structure as an example of 'exchanging ma-

terials for brains', and clearly expressed that the development of glass structures stems from an intellectual challenge. Due to delays in the overall building scheme of the shop, the curtain wall was only installed in February 1990. The drawing shows the dramatic effect the glass wall has spatially as a suspended transparent membrane even better than the photographs, as transparent glass structures are very hard to photograph clearly.

Biology Museum, Leiden

Architect Fons Verheijen designed a new Museum for Natural History in Leiden in 1989. One of the elements is a bridge 50 m long, 12 m high and 4 m wide for pedestrian use, connecting the existing renovated section of the museum with a new section, over the entrance road to the 'biological brain park'. As a symbol the skeleton of a whale was chosen to be suspended inside the bridge volume (fig 48). After one of the publications on the progress of the author's experiments, the architect contacted him by telephone, and the immediate result was the proposal to build the glass walls of the bridge in the structural glass system with compression studs and tension rods, but entirely on the outside of the bridge volume this time, not to conflict physically with the whale's skeleton. As a trial a smaller prototype of 7.2 x 3.6 m was installed, with metal components in the same system, suspended from the ceiling of the renovated section of the museum in order to convince future sponsors of the form design would take in the future. This time the skeleton of a killer whale was suspended behind the glass plane, visible in fig 49.

Curtain wall in Dubai

A similar design in the form of the Cool Cat model described above was proposed by the author in January 1990 for the entrance hall of an office building in Dubai. The size of the glass fascia is 6 m wide and 20 m high (fig 50). The total height is divided into squares of 6 x 6 m. The vertical height is subdivided by horizontal space frame trusses 1 m high to transfer the dead weight to the concrete structure of six vertical panels of 1 x 1 m each. Stabilization against wind forces is by means of double counterspanning guy trusses to transfer wind compression and suction on the glass surface vertically to the space frame trusses and horizontally to the concrete substructure. The module for the glass was proposed by the architect as 1 x 1 m, but changed by the author to 1.5 x 1.5 m.

49 Trial assembly of a suspended wall 3.6 × 7.2 m made of eight glass panels prestressed by studs and guy rods for the Biology Museum in Leiden NL . Designed by Fons Verheijen and the author in the summer of 1989.

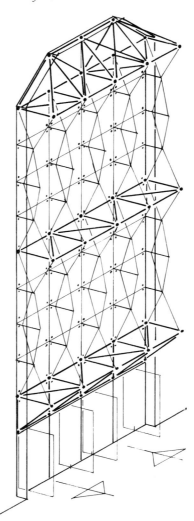

50 Design proposal drawings by the author (1990) for a curtain wall of an office building entrance hall in Dubai, using combinations of space trusses as main structures and underspanned glass panels.

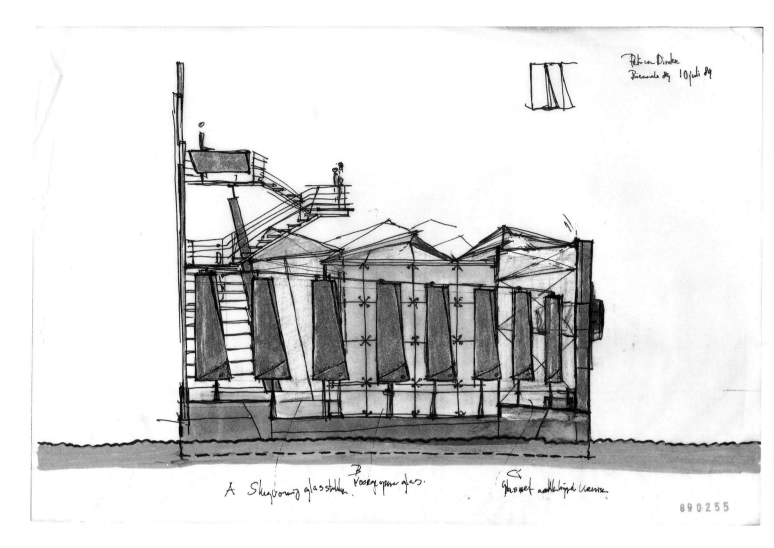

Floriade Follies, Zoetermeer

Architects are inspired by the minimal yet graphic design aspects of the developed structural glass walls, and are applying them in new designs. Young Dutch architect Peter van Dinter has used the Quattro glass system in the design of one of his 'de-constructivist' follies for the Zoetermeer Floriade 1992 (Netherlands). This design is an entry for the Young Dutch Architects' Biennale 1989 as sketched in fig 51. It confronts aeroplane wing-like sunscreens with the glass, obtaining a maximum contrast between movable closed volumes and a fixed transparent glass membrane.

51 Detail of elevation of Van Dinter's Follie with metal sunscreen wings and structural glass with Quattro nodes.

16 Glass Music Hall in the Berlage Exchange

The exchange of Berlage was built between 1898 and 1903 and was a building of prime architectural importance for its day. Apart from its renewing spatial and architectonical concept, Berlage used constructions in which materials were used optimally as to their properties; this fact must be seen as in a time when eclecticism in architecture prevailed. Berlage prepared the road for the Dutch Functionalists of the 1920s. His consistancy and his design have been inspiring. In the year 1990 architect Pieter Zaanen has followed much the same line of thought in all his renovations and adaptations of the exchange building to transform it into the current cultural centre. All interventions by Zaanen have been carefully kept separate from the original Berlage building, and have been realized in modern materials with a distinctly individual character. These interventions have been accomplished with much attention to detail – separate and yet connected. The Glass Music Hall has a strong character of its own and yet it exploits the Berlage building fully, making it host and parasite simultaneously. When Zaanen invited the author as a structural designer to develop his architectural concept of the Glass Music Hall further, it meant an oppor-

tunity for spatial structures of steel and glass to manifest themselves in this almost sacred place for architects where ninety years before Dr. Hendrik Petrus Berlage studied his materials and obtained optimal results from the then modern materials and technology. Responding to Zaanen's invitation would mean that our struggle to beat uncertainties (in short: 'product development') in our Quest for Structural Glass would be intensified. The only uncertainty at that time, during the construction of Berlage's building, was the subsoil condition, which shortly after completion required some adaptations to the building (such as tie bars between the steel trusses) and yet caused cracks in the brickwork walls in the course of time. Yet the exchange is more than worthwhile renovating. Nowadays it is a national cultural meeting point with its exhibition centre, accommodation of the NedPhO (the Dutch Philharmonic Orchestra) and the Grand Café Berlage. Two of the three large halls in the complex have been roofed by a saddle roof with ample glass surfaces: the former commercial exchange, now the cultural exhibition area and the former stock exchange, now the Wang concert hall with 600 seats. These glass roofs have been built as double roofs, where glass technology as developed in the 19th century was applied and truly integrated in the building. Todate the glass roofs of Berlage's building are world-famous and believed to form one of the roots of the current atrium mania for covered offices and hotels. The former grain

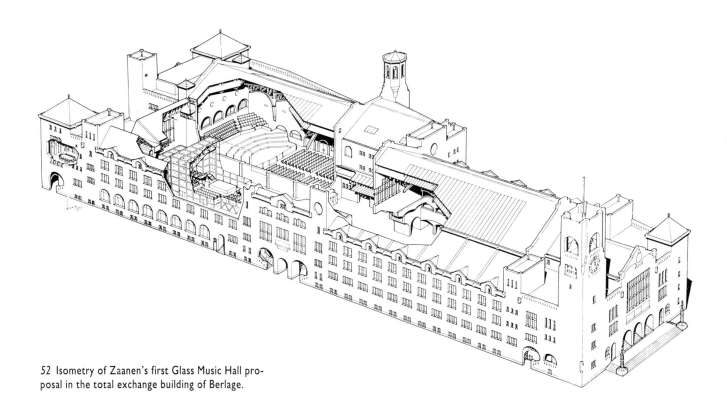

52 Isometry of Zaanen's first Glass Music Hall proposal in the total exchange building of Berlage.

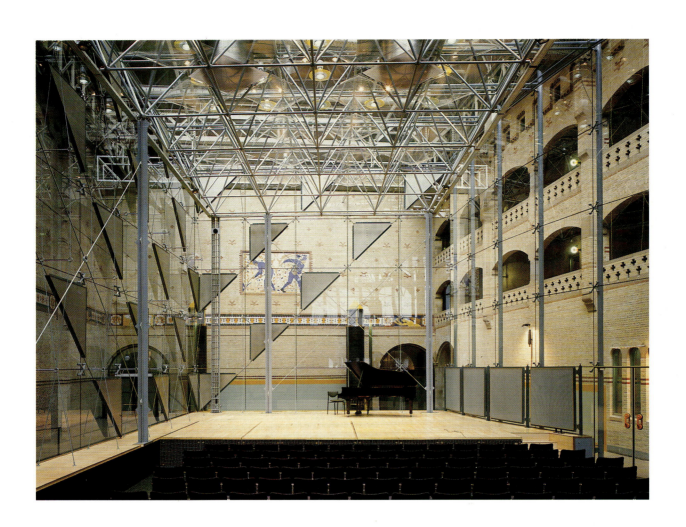

exchange has a different roof structure conceived as a system of flat riveted trussed girders in two directions on which five one-sided shed roofs have been placed. The presence of the many Polonceau-like secondary shed trusses gives the roof space a complex character. Contrary to the two saddle roofs, these shed skylights have been singly glazed. The internal volume of this former grain exchange measures 19 x 38 m, with a clear height of 16 m. The space itself is enclosed by three yellow brick walls with a continuous decorative ceramic frieze by the well-known Dutch artist Jan Toorop. The fourth wall has arched openings in front of a gallery behind which are offices.

Design Concept

It was in this same former grain exchange that the rehearsal space with chamber orchestra concert hall for the NedPhO was to be realized. The struggle the architect engaged in with the Cuypers Society, protector of the exchange as a monument (this building is one of the seven modern Dutch buildings on the official European list of architectural monuments), concerned their approval of building a new rehearsal space, as a completely freestanding space within the main space, with a 'temporary' character and if possible entirely of glass. This concept would solve the acoustic problem at the time of two simultaneous concerts in the Wang concert hall and the (Glass Music Hall or) Aga chamber music and rehearsal hall due to the relatively thin brick wall between the two adjacent concert halls. Moreover, it would solve the noise nuisance to and from the office gallery, and through the single glass roof skylights. The sound of trams and aeroplanes should hardly be heard inside. The ringing of the tower bells would still have to alternate with the music programmes. Within this concept of an independent all-glass hall in the existing building, Rob Metkemeyer of Peutz Associates (acoustic advisors) analysed that 8 mm of glass in the overall envelope would be sufficient to reduce the noise level by 24 dB. The design concept by Pieter Zaanen used to fight for building permission is illustrated in the isometric drawing of fig 52. After the first attempt to construct the Glass Music Hall with 9 m long ribbed glass panels had come aground on financial grounds, contact with Octatube was renewed. There, meanwhile, the theoretical study of Rik Grashoff had been completed, resulting in a structural system of glass planes stabilized and stiffened by metal cross bars and tensile rods (see par 14). Supply and demand linked up quite well and the first design impulses resulted in a rectangular box of 2000 m³, completely composed of prestressed and stabilized tempered glass panels. The sizes of the box were to be approximately 20 x 10 m and 10 m high. Actually this volume is less than 20% of the volume of the total

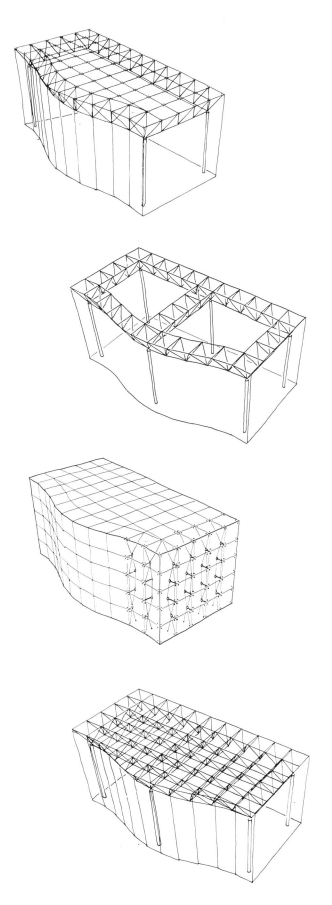

grain exchange, but has a completely different and much bigger visual impact. Some time later the box was given its special 'cello-like belly' to reduce 'flutter' effects between the two longer walls. While building a scale model Zaanen decided to place the glass volume obliquely in the grain exchange, optimizing the tension between glass volume and the total enclosing space, making the perception of entering the Aga Hall more exciting. The design concept was in fact very simply that of an assembly of glass plates, prestressed together to form five large glass planes. In this system tensile rods would introduce a compression force in the cross bars and in the glass planes. The roof plane was to be supported by the wall plane. External loadings perpendicular to the glass surface would result in more compression in the glass, a reduction of tension in the nearer tensile rod and a rise of tension in the remote tensile rod. In the roof, of course, the lower chord rods would have higher tensile stresses than the upper chord rods. The X-shape of the glass connecting node was developed to give a diagonal and spatial connection to the glass panels, especially in the roof plane; in the wall the forces would be more vertical (and a H-model would also be more appropriate but then again the result would be too like a copy of La Villette: simply 'not done'). The X-shape can be interpreted as a target – to try to achieve the horizontal glass roof structure one day. In anticipation of deflections of the glass due to the unknown creep and flow behaviour of tempered glass, the glass panels would be better suspended than stacked so that elongations could be post-tensioned and neutralized in future. After reviewing this proposal we realized it would be a very bold one, one requiring much experimentation before daring to have the glass roof supported by the glass walls. Perhaps too giant a step forward at that very moment. A more down-to-earth approach involved making four metal girder-like elements in the four roof corners, supported by vertical columns from and between which the separate glass planes were to be suspended. Ultimately the four metal roof elements were analysed as plane steel trusses; a 45° slope would make the trusses less visible from inside. The size of the upper and lower chord members was to be 250 mm, and each truss welded, posing a problem of transport and erection as the entrance doors allow only sections of max. 2 x 2m to enter the hall (see fig 53). All transport was to be done manually, hindered too by steep entrance stairs. After this proposal and a visit by the architect to the Octa laboratory where both the mock-up of a prestressed glass system (see fig 44) and the Cool Cat full-size trial assembly were erected, Zaanen set his mind definitively on an improvement of the structural scheme in architectural terms, by having both counterspanning mechanisms located on the inside of the glass planes, leaving the outside all glass, flush and abstract. All steel elements inside and slick glass

53 Different schemes for the Glass Music Hall as developed subsequently during the design process between architect and structural designer.

outside. The counterspanning tensile trusses would stabilize the free lower chord members of the flat trusses supporting the glass planes in their turn. A very daring interactive structural proposal, not in the least because deflection in the steel frames could cause serious deformations in the glass planes and perhaps cracks in glass plates. The relative large size of the truss elements led to an alternative of triangular trusses with much improved torsional stability and lighter diameter elements, built up as a lightweight space frame on six supports, from which the glass walls could be suspended and between which in the two large roof openings the underspanned roof glass plane could be installed. The tensile rods would not affect or influence the stability of the main delta trusses. Being essentially a space frame system, the delta trusses could be built up of manually bolted elements on site with few transport problems. Assembly by hand and hoisting with no accessibility for mobile cranes would have to be performed suspended from the roof trusses. All forementioned proposals would have meant a international novelty in the structural sense by the structural use of glass planes in the flat roof areas. The last proposal was rejected by the architect because of its hybrid character. All proposals were refused by the fire prevention officer as 30 minutes' fire resistance was required by him although no more than the equivalent of 5 kg wood (equal to 5 minutes) was present in the interior. In all, these advanced schemes were abandoned for three reasons:

• The fire prevention officer did not agree with the use of compressed horizontally laminated glass panels, held in position by only four corner glass brackets, and stabilized by short compression studs and thin tensile guy rods. An intermediate solution – to change from a purely underspanned glass structure to underspanned steel mullions, where the mullions are loaded under compression and the glass panels loaded on local bending moments – was vetoed by the architect as being hybrid. The architect's approach has been very consistent, something which was a particular stimulus to the design and development process.

• The estimated costs of the development of an entirely new area of building technology were much higher than those of the final design, because of the theoretical research and practical tests scheduled. Even with the project subsidy received by the NedPhO from the Ministry of Economic Affairs for Material Innovation, these costs were too high.

• The time required for the development of a trustworthy system of loadbearing glass panels in the horizontal roof would have extended the building schedule by another six months.

These were the reasons that this one big step forward – the realization of a real structural glass roof – could not be achieved in this project. Going back to the roots of architec-

ture and construction, the essence of making space has to do with laying floors, erecting walls and spanning roofs. In general walls are visually more important than floors, but roofs over spaces can give space a spatial impression and special character. So by developing the glass walls first, we followed this ancient path: it has always been easier to build floors and walls than to build roofs. Roofs require even more skill and ingenuity than walls. History is filled with examples of roofs that collapsed during or shortly after construction. So in 1989 we were satisfied for the time being only to make technical progress on the vertical wall structures. These walls could be realized without any objections from the authorities. The above reasons led to a simple stereotyped Tuball space frame, originally filling the complete roof area, thus including the curved belly part. For us space frames are conservative and reliable structural systems which by their static indeterminacy have the complete trust of the fire brigade officers, so that no extra provisions had to be taken to meet the required fire resistance.

The structural concept of the author was initially to have both the four wall planes and the roof plane composed as one integral glass plane built up of smaller individual tempered 1.8 x 1.8 m glass plates connected by means of the special X-shaped Quattro nodes diagonally, stabilized and stiffened by cross bars and tensile rods. In order to stabilize the glass planes against deadweight and external loadings, the Quattro joints on both sides of the glass panels would be connected with cross bars, the tops connected with adjustable tensile rods. This mechanism, like the Cool Cat wall, was proposed for application to both sides of the glass systematically, and on all four walls of the box. In order to dramatize the difference between the straight and the curved wall the architect decided to keep the space frame in the roof rectangular and to span the belly area with separate purlins. Also he decided not to use the stabilized system for the curved wall, but to stabilize it with thirteen exterior CHS columns, supported on lower brackets from the reinforced concrete foundations, suspended and detailed as organ pipes. The Quattro nodes in the curved wall have been welded with short distance keepers to the columns, in a rotated position according to the curve and with geometrical deviations from the norm.

This broad description of the design process clarifies how during the process architectonic and structural considerations mutually influenced each other, without too fixed a design idea in the mind of both designers. The open relationship between them led, due to their mutual contrast, to collisions and appraisals and has been experienced as a positive stimulant for the quality of the design.

• Transparency and counterlight. These two words are dependent on the light seen by the visitor: light from the back or from the front. In glass structures it means transparency and visible coloured metal joints and, above all, lit external walls and external masses. Or counterlight, with dark minimal metal skeletons in silhouette and gleaming light. Light has always been very important to glass.

• Colour. Grey-tinted glass plays on top of this a further, double role: seen from the outside with light directed on the ouside walls it could become completely black, while light on the inside could turn grey glass into transparent glass. Lit outside and unlit inside means that the grey tint disappears completely.

• Mirror and soap bubble. The mirror action of the glass is clearly visible from the back; with counterlight it disappears completely. The curvature in the fourth wall, the glass roof and the three square walls make distinctions between reflection and reality difficult. Berlage's building is mirrored and present everywhere. The orchestra seems to be playing in the roof.

Glass forms a minimally visible, maximally transparent envelope around a three-dimensional space that depending on the lighting can suddenly vanish like a soap bubble. The grey tint is like a chameleon and the glass structures like the King's new suit of clothes. These aspects can be observed in the Glass Music Hall in the former Exchange of Hendrik Petrus Berlage in Amsterdam.

The original proposal was to give the curved wall a grey tint, leaving the other three walls in clear glass (see fig 54). This would have resulted in a grey-tinted curved wall meandering in space. The reaction of the architect was even more sensitive: to have the three rectangular walls in grey and the curved wall in clear glass. On entering the hall the effect is a powerful one: walking towards a black box along a black wall, one opens the door and suddenly sees a space without a back wall – the transparent curved wall with Berlage's brickwork behind it. An architectural surprise, to be sure. Another surprise is when the lights in the Glass Hall are switched off, and the spotlights on the Berlage brickwork walls are on, there is hardly any visible difference between grey-tinted and clear glass: the glass just does not seem to be there at all: one is really in the original Berlage building. Walking around the Glass Hall means that one experiences the grey walls as a Black Box.

Wall Panels

The three straight walls are built as suspended glass walls, true curtain walls: all glass panels are suspended one under

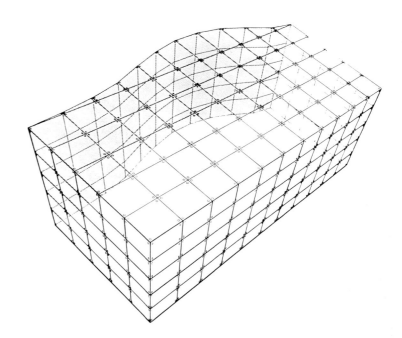

54 Bird's-eye view of the Glass Music Hall in Amsterdam, 9/13/10.8 m wide, 9 m high and 21.6 m long. Main structure is a flat space frame covered with glass panels of 1.8 × 1.8 m. The four walls are suspended curtain walls, doubly stabilized and composed of glass panels of 1.8 × 1.8 m.

the other. The highest panel carries the dead weight of all lower panels; the upper bolt holes have the greatest stresses. The acoustic requirement for the minimum thickness of 8 mm offered the suspended panels enough structural safety. Each glass panel has been suspended from two bolt holes in a bolt hole of dia. 20 mm at 100 x 100 mm distance from the four corners. The connecting glass brackets are each built up of four solid props diagonally connected by welded strips. On this cross of diagonal strips (or X-node) a perpendicular stud has been welded to transfer compression forces to the two tensile bars. The totality of this stabilizing system ensures the spatial stability of the glass panels against overpressure and underpressure.

The glass panels have been connected to the bracket by means of a pre-tension type of connection, provided with an extra friction layer. The bolt is an Allen-type countersunk high-tensile bolt in stainless steel 316. This pre-tensioning produces a connection with enough shear force to suspend the desired dead weight. Tests in the Octatube laboratory have shown that this type of connection has higher values (16 kN for M12 bolt by pre-tensioning) than the flush-type joints used by Pilkington in the United Kingdom and by Boussois in the conservatories of the 'Cité de la science et du

technique' in La Villette, Paris, as designed by Peter Rice et al (8 kN for M12 bolt by shear).

This nodal system was called the 'Quattro system' because of the four circular connection props, on the occasion of finding a motto for an innovative material-development competition held by the Dutch Ministry of Economic Affairs in 1990. The Quattro system was awarded the second price. This stabilizing system has been developed to have a guyed structure with both counterspanning directions on the inside of the glass. Counterspanning guy rods in two directions, outward and inward, are necessary because of the changing loading conditions of overpressure and underpressure from the air-conditioning system in the Glass Music Hall, and possible forces exerted by visitors on the lower panels. In this project no full wind load has been calculated that could act on a similar object outside. In such cases the glass panels would be 10 to 12 mm thick and the rods would also be slightly thicker. The glass panels in the walls measure 1.8 x 1.8 m, and have been produced as single tempered grey-tinted glass panels of 8 mm thickness. The safety of the glass panels and their resistance to any form of mechanical damage is of course the same as normal tempered glass as applied in shop windows, doors and squash wall panels. During the installation one of the upper panels was shattered by the mechanical tools of the installation crew, while the lower panels were already fixed. The collapse of this one upper panel left the other panels still suspended, so our theory of the 'square chainline' as an extra safety mechanism worked: the dead weight of the panels below the shattered panel were taken over by the adjacent panels. The upper bolt connections were calculated to take this load, 1.5 times greater than normal. The collapse of the upper panel did not lead to a progressive collapse, which was a personal relief to the author: one of the many technical doubts had been removed.

Acoustic Behaviour

Acoustic tests by Rob Metkemeijer who fired a pistol five times with blank cartridges, did not create visible trembling in the structure. Nor did 'high C' prove dangerous to the tension in the glass. After these acoustic tests many of the author's uncertainties and doubts were dispelled and the safety of the curtain walls was shown to the client to be adequate.

During installation the 8 mm thick glass panels proved to form a true curtain wall. At that time, the glass was not yet sealed in the joints and not yet fully prestressed by the counterspanning guy trusses. It appeared that the walls trembled easily and, for the author, even to an alarming degree. But after proper pretensioning and complete sealing

with black silicone sealant a thin but nevertheless reasonably stable wall was formed which functions acoustically as a 'flexible' wall. As mentioned before, the fourth wall has a curved plan to prevent flutter between the two larger parallel walls. Additional acoustic provisions made in the interior takes the form of (square and) triangular sound-absorbing panels of perforated aluminium sheets in natural colour with yellow fibreglass filling. The pattern of these panels has been so designed by the architect that the glazed character of the interior is reduced only minimally, but actually is felt more intensively. (Zaanen: 'naked beauty is felt stronger when partially concealed'). The curved wall has been decorated by six white spatially curved sails with a hard reflective GRP inner side and an absorbent fibreglass outer side.

The resulting acoustics are generally praised by musicians and critics, although slight differences in the hardness of the glass space are experienced at rehearsals and in concerts, with only a quartet playing or a full chamber orchestra of 25 musicians. The sound absorption surfaces are to be made more adaptable.

Erection and Installation

During installation of the glass panels their accuracy proved to be more than adequate. The glass panels were manufactured by the Swiss Securit factory, with the help of a computer-aided cutting and grinding machine, giving accuracies like $+0.0/-1.0$ mm in the orthogonal and diagonal directions; the bolt holes were cut by a water laser jet with even more refined accuracies: $+0.0/-0.2$ mm. Some small mistakes in the supplied glass could not be prevented, but were made by human errors and were clearly distinguishable. The accuracy of the glass panels was in fact so high that the normal accuracies of the space frame in which we at Octatube take such pride, looked quite rough and ready in comparison. Per panel the inaccuracies were no more than 2 mm at one place and had to be accommodated by drilling the bolt hole-filling nylon rings with eccentric holes invisible from the outside. It warned us, however, that the magnitude of these inaccuracies was quite unlike that normally observed on a building site. The space frame proved to be a very rigid structure without noticeable vertical deflections caused by the pre-tensioned guy trusses, which would have presented us with problems in aligning the horizontal seams of the glass plates. However, many man-hours were spent positioning the panels exactly, in order to get neat joint crossings: maximum deviation of the 9 mm joint was to be $+1.0/-1.0$ mm, yet still in total 2 mm maximum. So when working on this architectural objective, very high demands were put on the installation crew. The one-sided steel structure allowed for a more easy assembly than the original two-sided Cool Cat concept. Installation of the roof and wall panels was assisted by a maintenance bridge designed to be installed with a hoisting cat and vacuum suckers. The same type of vacuum suckers was used for the entrance door handles. Yet in general the scheduled building time was met, the building being completed in January 1990. Regular maintenance of the glass panels was scheduled, especially for the roof, as dust collects easily and all the internal lighting of the Glass Music Hall is suspended above the roof and the maintenance bridge. From a valuable suggestion by Ned-PhO's Willem Leopold, responsible for building and exploitation of the Aga Hall, the strips in the Quattro node were kept at a distance of 20 mm from the glass to leave at least reasonable access for the window cleaners.

By way of feedback to the original set-up of the true underspanned glass roof structure the author feels that six months extra for development, refinement and additional tests would have been very practical. The realized Glass Music Hall is a tribute to the great master Berlage in its honest modern material usage, the production techniques, the intelligent and yet simple static systems and the visual detailing. Berlage realized his building almost ninety years earlier, but its inspiration influenced the set-up and detailing of the Glass Music Hall to a great extent.

Technically the realization of the Glass Music Hall meant an important step forward. Though a number of uncertainties and doubts have been removed, some have been replaced by other difficulties, so that much work still needs to be done and the Glass Music Hall can be seen as only one single step ahead in the Quest for Glass Space Structures. Moreover, the main goal seen at the start of the design – to realize horizontal underspanned glass roofs with almost invisible metal components, truly defying gravity – had not been reached here, but would be only later, as described in par 20. Despite these considerations of technical progression and despite the very minimal consumption of steel, the Glass Music Hall has been nominated for the Dutch Steel Price 1990.

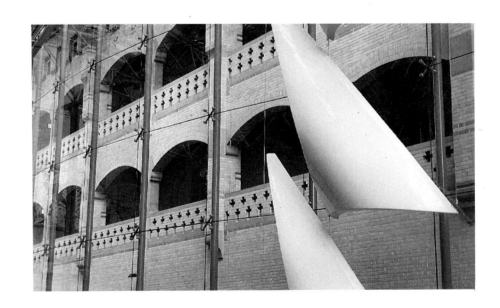

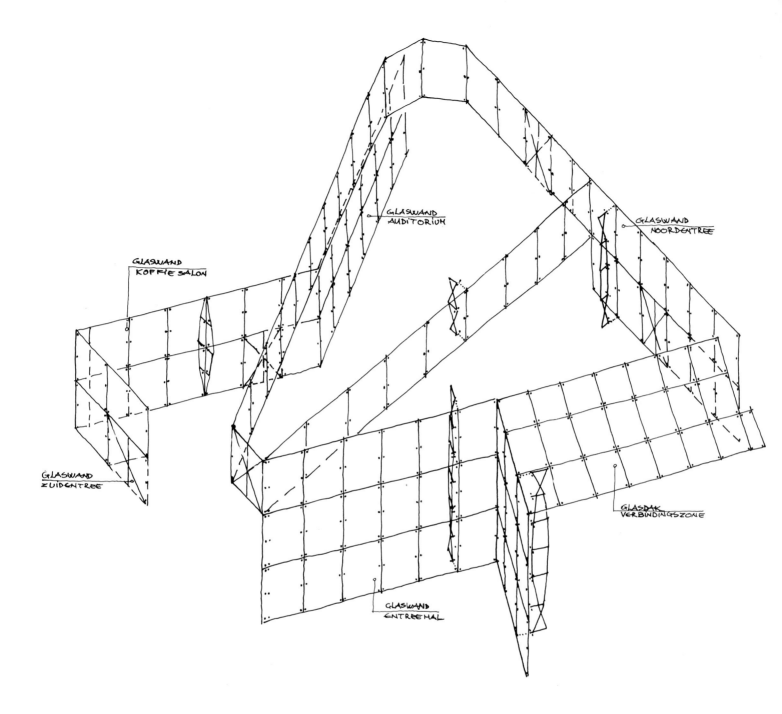

GLASWAND
KOFFIE SALON

GLASWAND
AUDITORIUM

GLASWAND
NOORDENTREE

GLASWAND
ZUIDENTREE

GLASWAND
ENTREEHAL

GLASDAK
VERBINDINGSZONE

63 Design sketches for the fascia glass structure of
the Dutch Architectural Institute in Rotterdam.

17 Dutch Architectural Institute, Rotterdam

In 1988 a limited design competition for the Dutch Architectural Institute in Rotterdam was won by Prof. Jo Coenen. He described his design as follows: 'It consists of five elements: an extended archive building, a square exhibition space, a low entrance with obliquely above the administrative building an enormous pergola which hangs over the building and makes it powerfully expressive'. (Hans Ibelings, *Jo Coenen, the Discovery of Architecture* Rotterdam 1989). The central entrance area is the hinge between different buildings, being made of various materials and having different directions and levels. The full complexity of the building is expressed in the entrance area. Hence the architect wished to enclose this volume with a transparent skin. After a number of direct and open discussions a structural principle for the walls was adopted similar to that realized in the Music Glass Hall, i.e. for vertical walls 3 m, 6 m and 9 m high that form flat or curved fascias (fig 63). The target is to realize these walls in insulated glass, silicone sealed; at the seams will be a visible black line maximum 10 mm wide. The individual glass panels measure 1.5 x 3.0 m and have six connection points, four at the corners and two in the middle of the longer sides. These points are connected by Quattro-node brackets, horizontal studs and counterspanning solid bars. The glass panels are hence supported at a distance of 1.5 x 1.5 m, forming vertical guy trusses every 1.5 m. The glass panels are all suspended between the substructures above and below. In most cases these are steel elements. In the case of reinforced concrete, which is subject to creep over a period of two years, an additional steel element will be fitted in-between, with the possibility of adjusting it vertically should the deformation of the substructure indeed occur to that extent. A major consideration is the outlook of the glass curtain wall in detail: out of visual considerations of minimum seam width the architect has set his mind on single rather than double glass. However for reasons of insulation double glazing will also be developed, complete with the 'pièce de résistance': the puncturing of the Quattro node through the double glass panels and the air space in-between, the most difficult problem to be solved structurally (compression forces by prestressing) and technically (keeping this penetration airtight). The disadvantage of using double glass units sealed together is that visually the joints form a black line of 35 to 40 mm wide, even without covering aluminium strips. Moreover the double glass sealant joints will have to be covered by metallic strips to combat UV light. Single glass joints however have only a width of 10 mm. The structure of the metal components are used to unify the very different parts of the glass

envelope around the central entrance. The connection between entrance and exhibition building will be made by a transparent structural glass roof, stabilized by counterspanning guy rods and studs, making the involvement of the two building volumes clear to the professional observer. To complicate a simple design even further, this roof will be punctured by two of the vertical columns of the multi-storey office block above. Realization of these glass structures is scheduled for 1991.

18 Glass Cubes and Pyramids

Just after the technical feasibility study described in par 14, and a few months before the design of the Glass Music Hall, a cluster of outdoor exhibition pavilions was designed in 1988 by architect Wiek Röling and the author for the Centraal Museum in Utrecht, the Netherlands.

Centraal Museum, Utrecht

The cluster consisted of a number of identical glass cubes, each composed of a compressed cubic form built up of square glass panels of 2.1 x 2.1 m, with flush outside surfaces and counterspanning guy systems on the inside. The project remained unrealized for financial reasons, but the results had a stimulating effect on the development process described in this book. The main step forward here was a belief in the ability to develop a horizontal guyed roof constructed of glass panels (fig 64). After the realization of the Glass Music

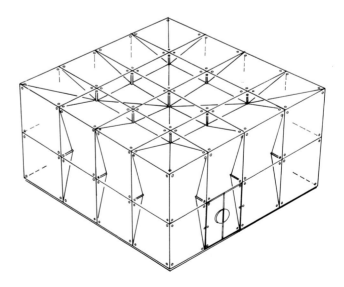

64 Glass exhibition pavilion for the Centraal Museum in Utrecht, designed by architect Wiek Röling and the author in 1988 as a glass cube composed of square heat-strengthened glass panels of 2.1 × 2.1 m stabilized by internal cross bars and counteracting tensile rods.

Hall it was felt that all-glass structures require a similarly high degree of workmanship on the site, and that temporary buildings in such systems would prove very expensive.

Flower Pavilion, Rotterdam

In February 1990 a design proposal was made by the project architects Cas Oosterhuis and Ton van Hoorn for a flower-shop pavilion of 12 x 12 m in the well-known Lijnbaan shopping centre in Rotterdam. This object (fig 65) will replace a smaller shop. The design is conceived as four joined steel cubes each 6 x 6 x 6 m, bordered with steel RHS/CHS ribs 6 m apart. The wall and roof planes are 6 x 6 m, subdivided into vertical distances of 2 m (to accommodate entrance doors) and 1.5 m in the horizontal direction to minimize buckling lengths in the glass panels. All planes have counterspanned glass panels, double glass in the roof, and single in the walls (to have minimal reflection for its shop function). The glass panels in the lower wall areas can be removed as toughened glass doors.

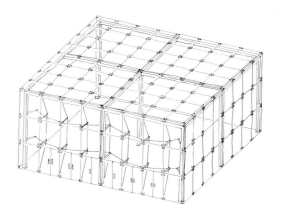

65 Design proposal drawings of a flower shop (12 × 12 × 6 m) in the Lijnbaan shopping centre in Rotterdam (1990).

Drayton Park Pyramid, London

Since the excitement generated by I.M.Pei's pyramid at the Louvre in Paris, many pyramid proposals have been sketched by architects these last two years. One of the smaller examples is an atrium pyramid for an office building in London. It has been designed by Rob Loader of Evans & Shalev Architects for an office development at Drayton Park in London (see figs 66). The size of the pyramid is 7.8 x 7.8 m, with a summit height of 3.9 m. The pyramid is composed of single clear tempered glass panels with a side length of 1.9 m in rhombic and triangular panels. The glass panels are stabilized on the lower side to the substructure, and on the four ribs to each other. Only three nodes in the middle of the faces of the pyramid required extra stabilizing perpendicular to the glass plane. The architect's proposal was to use an external space frame, but alternative proposals to use only three bars per side to stabilize the three middle points and have the other nodes stabilized by the glass itself, led to the final proposal to cover the three middle points with a tepee-like structure of two tubes crossing on each face in an X-shape. The 'tepee' structure runs now exactly in line with the glass seams. The 4 x 3 middle points have the same Quattro-node details as in Amsterdam, adapted to their current function and slightly altered geometrically. The structure outside the glass means that the glass surface on the inside is flush and that all glass panels are suspended. In winter the danger of frost in the suspension details is avoided by rubber watertight rings on the outside and ample space (30 mm) for cleaning the glass panels from the outside.

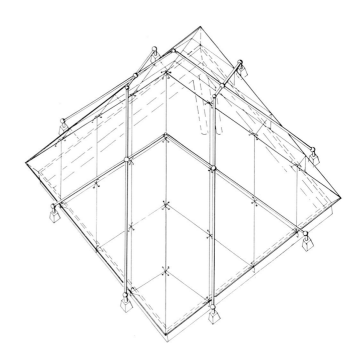

66 The Drayton Park pyramid: single glass supported by an external tepee-like structure, built as a High-Tech sophisticated element in this office courtyard, surrounded by curtainwalling. The pyramid is the rooflight for the reception area of this office complex, with black marble flooring, reflecting in the glass.

19 Glass Umbrellas

The first application truly designed as a glass structure in a roof surface in the course of the Quest for Structural Glass was the pedestrian bridge in an exhibition project known as the 'House of the Future' built in Rosmalen, the Netherlands.

House of the Future, Rosmalen

In this house all kinds of new materials and building techniques were experimented with, largely paid for by the contributing companies. The overall design of the House of the Future was by architect Cees Dam, using the ideas of Chriet Titulaer, the Dutch space scientist and advocate of futuristic techniques. The design of the pedestrian bridge over a pond between the actual house and an audiovisual exhibition room, was made by the author in 1989, and is illustrated by the isometric drawing in fig 67. The structure consists of two roofs of umbrella-like units, each composed of a vertical steel column and four glass plates 15 mm thick, and stabilized in both upward and downward directions by guy rods fixed at the corners of the glass plates like those of the Cool Cat wall. The architect chose transparent glass plates; the author's original idea was to make them grey or screen-dotted and more visible and give more the impression of an umbrella for people leaving the audiovisual room. The design also required a glass-blasted translucent laminated 20 mm glass floor and a 10 mm glass balustrade. The total size of the bridge is 8 x 4 m in plan. As the author was only invited to take part at a very late phase, the design had to be adapted to provisions for columns already poured into the concrete, giving cause for the modular design, whereas a linear design would have been appropriate but impossible to tie in with the provisions already made. The development of this design was assisted by the TNO Research Institute at Delft who however were very cautious and conservative in their advice on thickness and type of glass and lamination, and who advised against the use of merely tempered glass in the roof plane. Their proposal of double-laminated tempered glass panels resulted in too high a price which the project sponsor Veromco could not afford. Due to time limits the solution therefore was to build a metal framework and to simply have laminated glass sealed to the steelwork allowing replacement by structural glass panels in the future. TNO then withdrew from the project. So once the bridge had been realized and the House officially opened, the desired step of building a structural glass roof had yet to be taken.

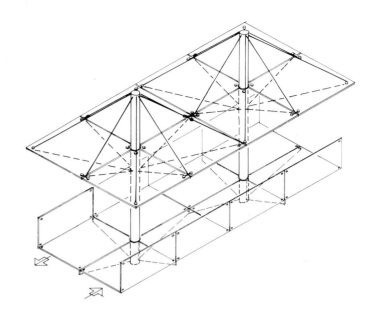

67 Isometric diagram of the pedestrian bridge of the 'House of the Future', composed of two umbrellalike glass elements and a glass floor.

Glass Parasol

Later in 1990 a prototype of a 4 x 4 m parasol composed of four horizontal glass plates 2 x 2 m cantilevering from one central steel pole, was built and tested in the Octatube laboratory, functioning as a grey-tinted glass umbrella (fig 68), for later use as an atrium garden parasol for the author's new house in Delft. It was by building it and showing that it worked (simply by loading it with sandbags) that doubts were conquered, and proof given that a thickness of 12 mm in single tempered glass panels was sufficient.

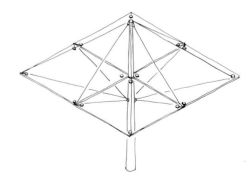

68 Prototype of a 4 × 4 m grey-tinted glass umbrella suspended from and prestressed on a central mast.

20 Flat Underspanned
Glass Roofs

The final stage in this report is the realization by the author of the first outdoor glass roof in a guyed structure. Not yet in a form where the cooperation of glass panels and metal underspanning is 100% actively structural, but rather passively so. The building's architect is Walter Lockefeer, a young Dutch architect working in Belgium and in the Netherlands in the tradition of Dom Hans van der Laan (founder of a Dutch architectural stream in which traditional materials and strict proportions combine in a very basic architecture). The design of the glass roof was made by the project architect and the author jointly, while the architect worked out the design in great detail in cooperation with the Octatube design team, making simultaneous models, computer graphics, detail designs and static analyses (fig 69) in our office.

The Flower Gate is a pavilion building in the archetypal form of a gate. The choice of an elementary design concept led to the pillars of the gate (the facades) being closed, unable to receive daylight. The chosen elementary building scheme is based on universal principles of form, and is in itself Low-Tech, confronted with a High-Tech roof. The origin of architecture is erecting vertical walls and horizontal roofs. The archetypal gate building is giving access symmetrically to a nursery for trees, plants and flowers; at the end of the plot, behind a 3 m high 40m wide brickwork wall with a central entrance, is the house of the De Wolf family, floriculturists. The glass roof on the gate shop illustrates the necessity of daylight for flowers.

Three alternatives have been investigated, designed and priced: a space frame supporting glass panels, an underspanned metal grid structure supporting glass panels and an underspanned Quattro roof. The outcome in all cases would be a horizontal glass roof. The architect and the client opted for the most intelligent, and most complicated last-named solution. The gate building is composed of two brickwork cubes 6.870 x 6.870 x 6.870 m, with an entrance bay of 2.230 m wide. The two cubes are entirely enclosed in the outer walls. The glass roof is at a height of 5 m, the remaining wall forming a parapet around it (see fig 70). The roof is completely composed of flat double-glass panels (comprising reflective tempered upper panels of 8 mm, a 12 mm air cavity and 3.3.1 laminated clear glass for the lower panels). The total size of the roof is 6.090 x 15.150 m; the individual panels measure 1.425 x 1.425 m. Each panel is supported at the four corners by support brackets designed in the same fashion as the Quattro nodes of the Glass Music Hall in Amsterdam. All suspended rods are stabilized against downward and up-

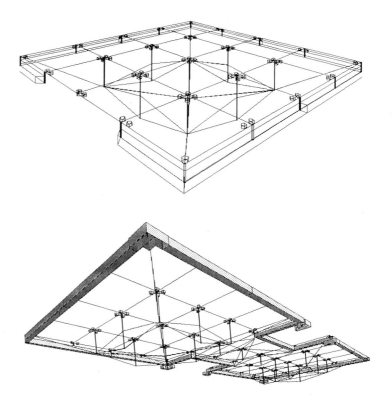

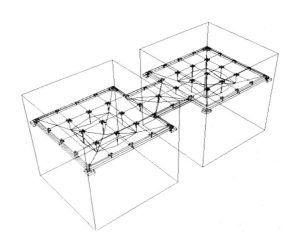

69 Perspective views of the glass roof structure in the two brick cubes of the Hulst Flower Gate, developed by architect Walter Lockefeer and the author in 1989.

70, 71 Detailled views of the realized underspanned glass roof for the Flower Gate in Hulst,
seen from above and below.

ward forces, and against asymmetrical loading. The Quattro nodes are glued to the laminated lower glass panels, with a detail allowing the support to be turned slightly in a vertical direction by means of deflecting rubber buffer cushions. At the same place the upper glass panel is also supported by a solid prop in the 12 mm air cavity, sealed between upper and lower panels. The steel support elements have been glued with a specially tested type of glue to the glass inner pane to give sufficient adherence for horizontal shear and vertical uplift. Each of the glass brackets has been extended with a vertical 20 mm thick pole guyed with 12 mm steel rods in the node as shown in fig 71. All tensile rods can be adjusted in length and tension. The whole structure is surrounded by a continuous RHS frame section supporting a continuous gutter. Hence this system can still be regarded as halfway between a closed roof system and an open structure with a perimeter ringbeam that takes the compression forces omitted in the upper glass panels and converts them into internal bending moments. The slope of the glass panels is 1%. The structure was completed in May 1990.

21   Glass Space Frames

The Quest for True Glass Structures still continues, getting increasingly closer to its goal of horizontal roof planes completely of glass where the glass is loaded by normal forces, instead of using the glass panels only as a secondary transparent cladding suspended from or fixed on a horizontal steel structure.

Fish-Belly Frames

For an atrium skylight for the Amro office in The Hague, the author advised project architect Maarten Grasveld in the spring of 1989, at his request, to design a glass structure 7 x 14 m in plan, with a fish-belly cross section, composed of an upper layer of glass panels (mainly under compression) and a lower layer (mainly under tension), with vertical intermediate bracing studs connecting the two layers with Quattro nodes on each side of the studs, and stabilized for asymmetrical loading by metal cross-bracing bars/cables (fig 72). The middle height should be some 2 m so that the space could be entered and used for heating, cooling and cleaning. This proposal was not realized, but serves as a guide for further development. If it were not so, this book would be open-ended.

Concertina-Glass Space Frames

One of the distinct disadvantages of the forementioned double-layered glass space frames, consisting of upper and

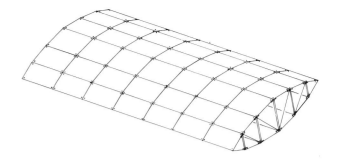

72 Isometry of the Amro bank atrium skylight at the Hague, in the form of a fish-bellied double-layered glass space structure, where glass panels form the compression and tension layer, while the metal tubes only function as connections and bracing.

lower chord glass panels and metal bracings, is that 50% of these glass panels are loaded under compression, and have an inefficiency caused by buckling of these plates. Two civil engineering students at Delft have devoted their final studies to developing a system without this buckling restraint in the glass: they are Rob Bakker and Gerald Lindner (June 1990). Their concept is in fact astonishing simple. Taking a double-layered glass space frame, with two glass planes and metal bracings, these bracings are arranged in a scissor-like topology. When this concertina arrangement is contracted perpendicular to the glass planes, it automatically stretches out in the plane of the glass, pre-tensioning the glass panels while most of the metal bracings are put under the resulting compression forces (fig 73). Pre-tensioning can be done half or fully depending on the magnitude of tensile stresses and eventual compression stresses resulting from the pre-tension loading case and the applied external loadings. This ingenious principle will be elaborated on at Octatube's in future projects in the coming years.

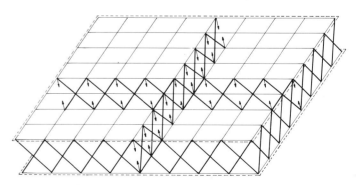

73 Prestressed Concertina-model in double layered space frame proposal where all glass plates have been prestressed by compressed bracings.

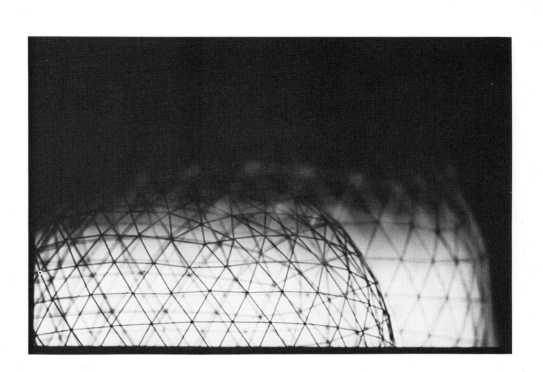

Biography

Adrianus Cornelis Jozef 'Mick' Eekhout, 1950
Married, two sons

Education
Highschool (HBS-b) St. Stanislas College, Delft 1962-1968
University of Technology in Delft, at the faculty of Architecture 1968-1973

Practical Work
Institut für leichte Flächentragwerke / Frei Otto, Stuttgart 1970
Renzo Piano, Genova 1970
Student Assistant 1971-1973

Graduation
October 1973 Cum Laude (Prof Jaap Oosterhoff / Prof Carel Weeber)

Doctor's degree
May 1989 Cum Laude (Prof Jaap Oosterhoff / Prof Moshe Zwarts (promotors);
Doctor's commission: Prof Dick Dicke / Prof Dr Zygmunt Makowski / Prof Dr
Stephan Polonyi / Prof Wiek Röling / Prof Ludwig van Wilder). Title
dissertation: 'Architecture in Space Structures'

Profession
1973 Computer analysis of space frames, TU Delft
1974 Architect at Groosman Partners Total Planning, Rotterdam
1974/1975 Architect at Thunissen, Van Kranendonk, Becka, The Hague

Architect
Independent office from Jan 1976-Jan 1982

Engineer
Octatube Engineering bv founded April 1978

Producer
Octatube Space Structures bv founded Dec 1983 (General Director)
The Octatube Group of Companies has several subsidiary companies in Delft
and abroad (UK, India, Singapore, Malaysia) and agencies abroad (Belgium,
Germany, Italy, Emirates, Hongkong). In 1990 Octatube had 50 employees in
Delft, amongst whom 20 architects and engineers, at Rotterdamseweg 200,
2628 AS Delft. Tel 31-15-571300/569362 Fax 31-15-622300

Lectures
From 1972-1990 regular lectures on space structures, structural design and
architecture etc at TU Delft, TU Eindhoven, Academies of Architecture in
Amsterdam, Rotterdam, Tilburg, Utrecht and NHIBS Antwerp.
Lectures delivered to professionals in the Netherlands and in Abu Dhabi,
Antwerp, Baltimore, Bombay, Brussels, Edinburgh, Kuala Lumpur, London,
New Dehli, Madras, Madrid, Milan, Singapore, Stuttgart and Sydney. Several
post-academic courses on aspects of structural design and architecture at
Delft 1985-1991.
Has written more than 60 articles in professional magazines of the
Netherlands and abroad.
Book 1 'Architecture in Space Structures' (dissertation) May 1989.
Monograph 'Aluminium in Ruimtelijke Constructies' March 1990.
Book 2 'Product Development in Glass Structures' October 1990.
Book 3 'Structural Design in Space Frames' scheduled for 1991.
Co-founder of Delft Design, Delft, December 1987.
Co-founder of Booosting, The Hague, August 1988.
On the board of several professional organisations:
Booosting; Staalbouwkundig Genootschap; Gipec.